Getting Started in
Radio Control Cars

by John Huber

from the publishers of
Radio Control
CAR ACTION

About the Author...

The first R/C car I ever drove was a Tamiya Toyota on-road car. I had to beg my friend to let me try it, and I repaid him by promptly smashing it into a curb. (He should have let me drive it in a more open parking lot!) That was back around 1980, and I must say that I've learned a lot since then. I bought my first car, a used Tamiya Sand Scorcher, about six years later. It was already very outdated (no diff, hardly any suspension and very heavy) but it was beefy enough for me to bash around for a couple months while I got used to how radios, servos, batteries and motors worked. I even added skis and spiked tires for winter!

My next car was a big step up. I bought a Tamiya 1/12-scale Toyota Toms—this time, new. It was designed for on-road racing and, for a year or so, it filled my need for speed. Wanting to go ever faster, I bought a 1/12-scale Fine Design dragster. Wow! Was it fast! When I scared a few joggers, I was promptly kicked off my high school track.

Around this time, I started to lose track of just how many cars I had. I got a job at a hobby shop and was building at least a kit a week. I started to race at a local carpet oval and got a taste for competition at about the same time. At least a couple of times a week, I went to the track with friends, and we had a blast chasing one another around the track. We made new friends and tried different styles and classes of racing. It was at this track that I met Steve Pond (the former editor of *Radio Control Car Action*) and started reading the magazine. I continued to race and eventually decided to send *Car Action* a letter and some photos of a car I had built. When Steve offered me a job, I was floored! I could do reviews of these cars and actually be paid for it?

Since then, I've worked as an associate editor and contributing author for *Car Action*, and I still love to build and modify cars in my basement speed shop. I hope that the information in this book helps you get as much out of this hobby as I have. I'm always interested in hearing from readers; please send your questions or comments to me via e-mail at JKHUBER@aol.com or jhuber@airage.com. And remember rule number one: have fun!

Getting Started in Radio Control Cars

Group Publisher
Louis V. DeFrancesco, Jr.

Group Editor-in-Chief
Tom Atwood

Special Publications Manager
Karen J. Huber

Copy Director
Lynne Sewell

Managing Art Director
Alan J. Palermo

Book Design
Michael Bouse

Director of Marketing
Gary Dolzall

Production Manager
Mary Reid McElwee

Copyright© 1995 by Air Age Inc.
ISBN: 0-911295-34-8
All rights reserved, including the right of reproduction in whole or in part in any form. This book, or parts thereof, may not be reproduced without the publisher's permission.
Published by Air Age Inc.,
251 Danbury Rd., Wilton, CT 06897.

PRINTED IN THE USA

Contents

Introduction 4

CHAPTER 1
Your First Car 5

CHAPTER 2
Electric Cars and Trucks 15

CHAPTER 3
Electric Motors and Gearing 23

CHAPTER 4
R/C Electronics 33

CHAPTER 5
Ni-Cd Batteries and Chargers 41

CHAPTER 6
Gas Cars, Trucks and Engines 49

CHAPTER 7
Basic Race Tuning 63

CHAPTER 8
Building, Painting and Detailing Your Model 73

CHAPTER 9
Hop-Ups and Modifications 83

CHAPTER 10
Troubleshooting 89

Index of Manufacturers 96
An alphabetical list of the companies asterisked throughout the book.

Introduction

Radio-control cars have changed quite a bit in the past 15 years. In this short time, cars have become faster and lighter, they run longer, and, best of all, they're more affordable. New car designs have emerged, as have new electronic and mechanical advancements. When I got started in R/C cars, they cost several hundred dollars, ran for about 10 minutes and were slow. And as if that wasn't enough, the only chargers available were overnight trickle chargers, so you could only run one pack a day! Not anymore...

Today, for less than $200, you can get a good beginner car with a radio, a battery and a charger, and its speed will be very good. If you're looking for a car to start with, don't bother looking at a toy-store variety. These cars aren't as fast, and spare parts aren't readily available. I recommend that you start with an off-road car, so that you'll be able to practice anywhere you want. With the strength of the materials used in cars today, you can do just about anything without damaging them. If you want to race, check to see whether there are tracks in your area. Chances are that people of all skill levels, with all types of cars, will be there. You'll fit in somewhere!

In this book, I'll tell you what you need to know to get started and how to make the most of the hobby. Remember, this is a hobby, and these cars aren't toys. The more time you spend tending to details in the pits, the fewer problems you'll encounter on the track. Good luck and have fun!

CHAPTER 1

Your First Car

- How they work
- Types of cars
- Tools
- Accessories you'll need
- Hobby shops and mail order

How they Work

Radio-control cars are very easy to operate. With most cars, you control two functions: steering and speed. You control them through your transmitter, which you hold in your hands. In the car, electronics convert your transmitted signals into throttle and steering movements that are in proportion to your original inputs. A device called a servo gives you control of the steering, and the throttle is controlled by an electronic or mechanical speed control. Though all the workings can get pretty complicated, the manufacturers have made all the parts modular, so they can be used with a variety of components.

I detail all the workings of the cars and accessories in the following chapters, but it would be a good idea to familiarize yourself with all the parts so that you'll know what I'm talking about. The following pages show some examples of types of R/C cars and their parts.

YOUR FIRST CAR

1/8-Scale 4WD Off-Road Gas Truck

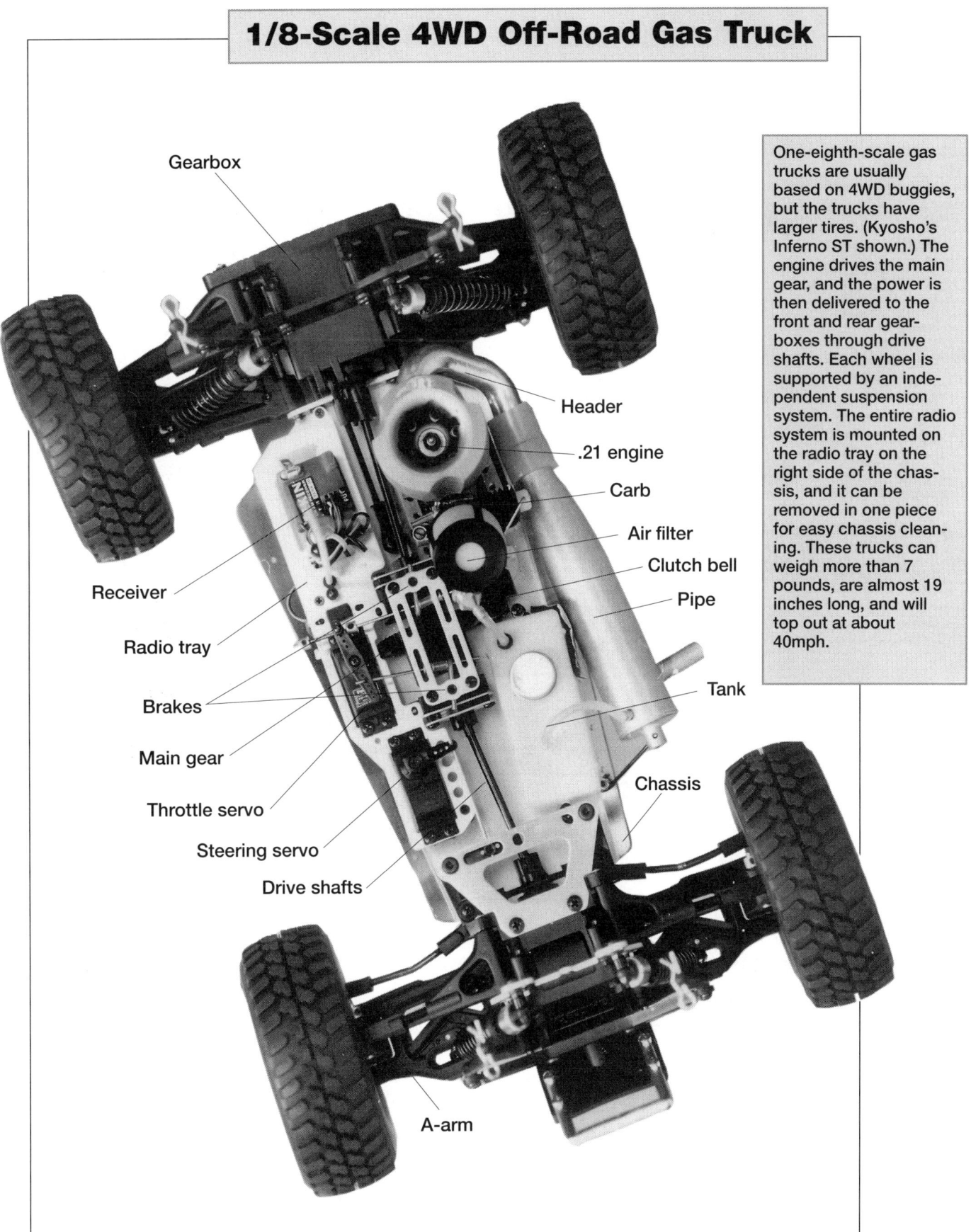

One-eighth-scale gas trucks are usually based on 4WD buggies, but the trucks have larger tires. (Kyosho's Inferno ST shown.) The engine drives the main gear, and the power is then delivered to the front and rear gearboxes through drive shafts. Each wheel is supported by an independent suspension system. The entire radio system is mounted on the radio tray on the right side of the chassis, and it can be removed in one piece for easy chassis cleaning. These trucks can weigh more than 7 pounds, are almost 19 inches long, and will top out at about 40mph.

CHAPTER 1

1/10-Scale 4WD On-Road Chassis

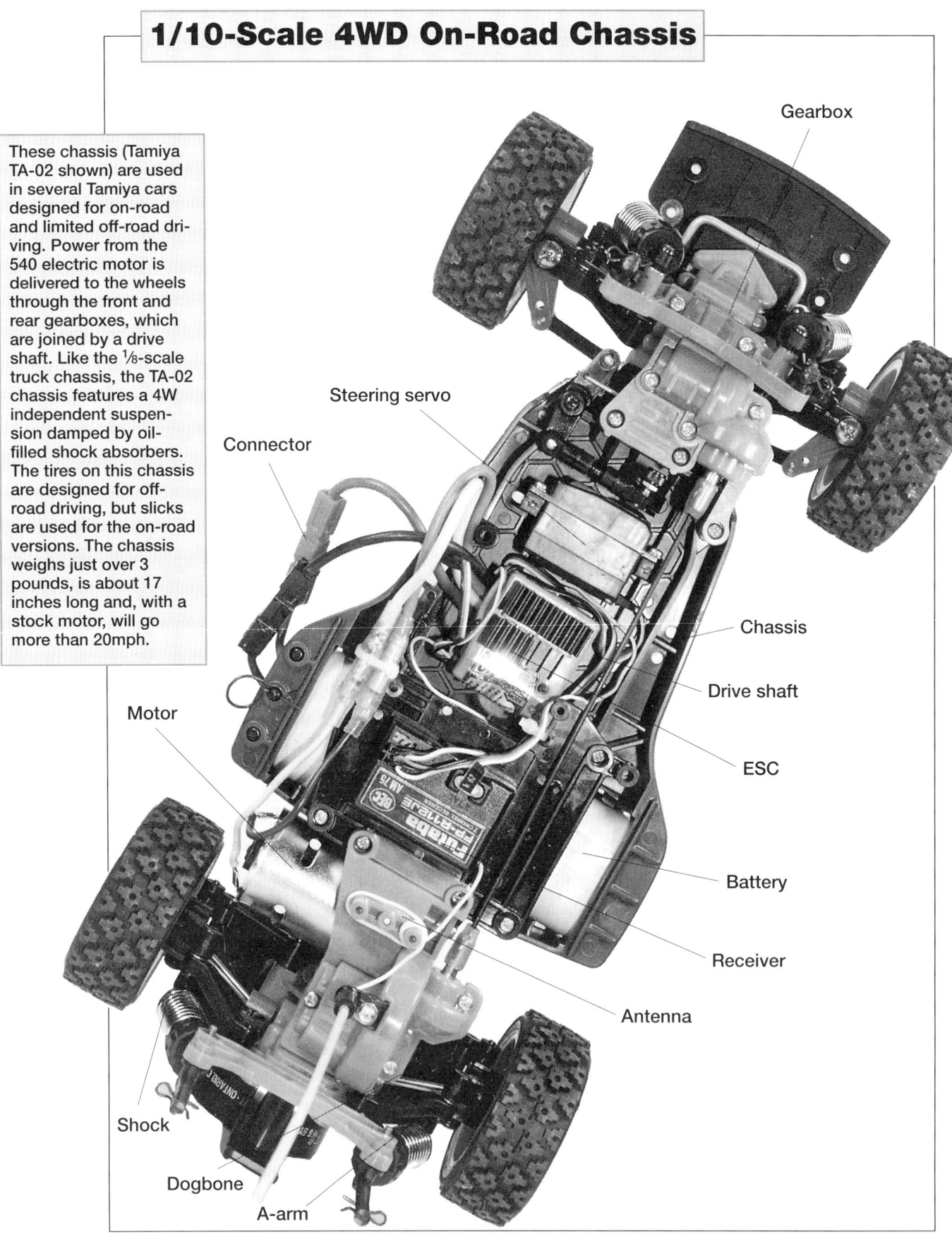

These chassis (Tamiya TA-02 shown) are used in several Tamiya cars designed for on-road and limited off-road driving. Power from the 540 electric motor is delivered to the wheels through the front and rear gearboxes, which are joined by a drive shaft. Like the 1/8-scale truck chassis, the TA-02 chassis features a 4W independent suspension damped by oil-filled shock absorbers. The tires on this chassis are designed for off-road driving, but slicks are used for the on-road versions. The chassis weighs just over 3 pounds, is about 17 inches long and, with a stock motor, will go more than 20mph.

YOUR FIRST CAR

1/10-Scale 2WD Off-Road Buggy

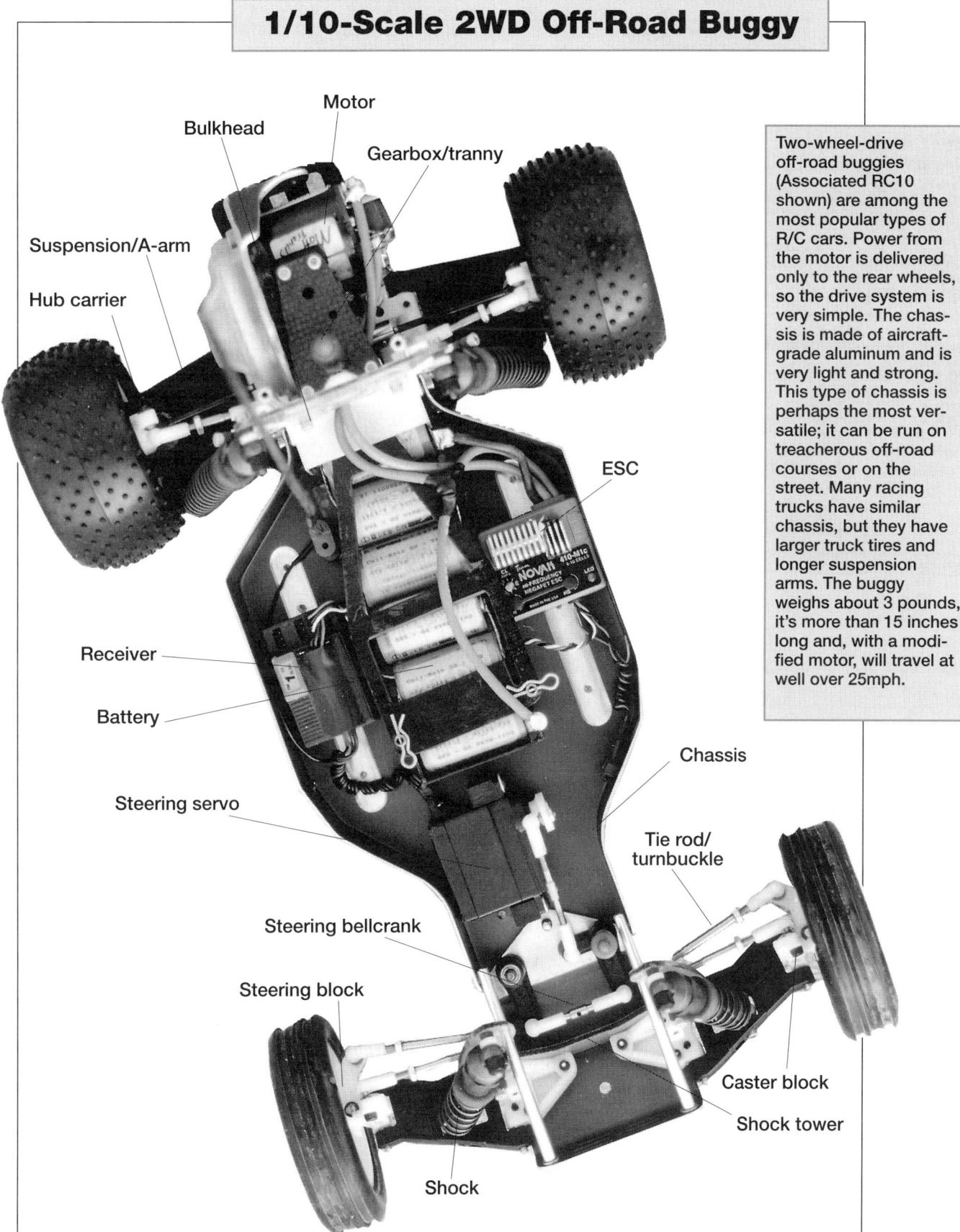

Two-wheel-drive off-road buggies (Associated RC10 shown) are among the most popular types of R/C cars. Power from the motor is delivered only to the rear wheels, so the drive system is very simple. The chassis is made of aircraft-grade aluminum and is very light and strong. This type of chassis is perhaps the most versatile; it can be run on treacherous off-road courses or on the street. Many racing trucks have similar chassis, but they have larger truck tires and longer suspension arms. The buggy weighs about 3 pounds, it's more than 15 inches long and, with a modified motor, will travel at well over 25mph.

CHAPTER 1

1/10-Scale 2WD Gas Off-Road Truck

This has evolved from 1/10-scale buggies. It has many of the same components as the buggies, but, as you can see, it has longer suspension arms and larger truck tires. The .12 engine is capable of cranking out just under 1 hp, which will propel the truck to speeds of more than 30mph. This truck weighs just over 4 pounds and is about 16 inches long. (Traxxas Nitro Hawk shown.)

10 GETTING STARTED IN R/C CARS

1/10-Scale 2WD On-Road Car

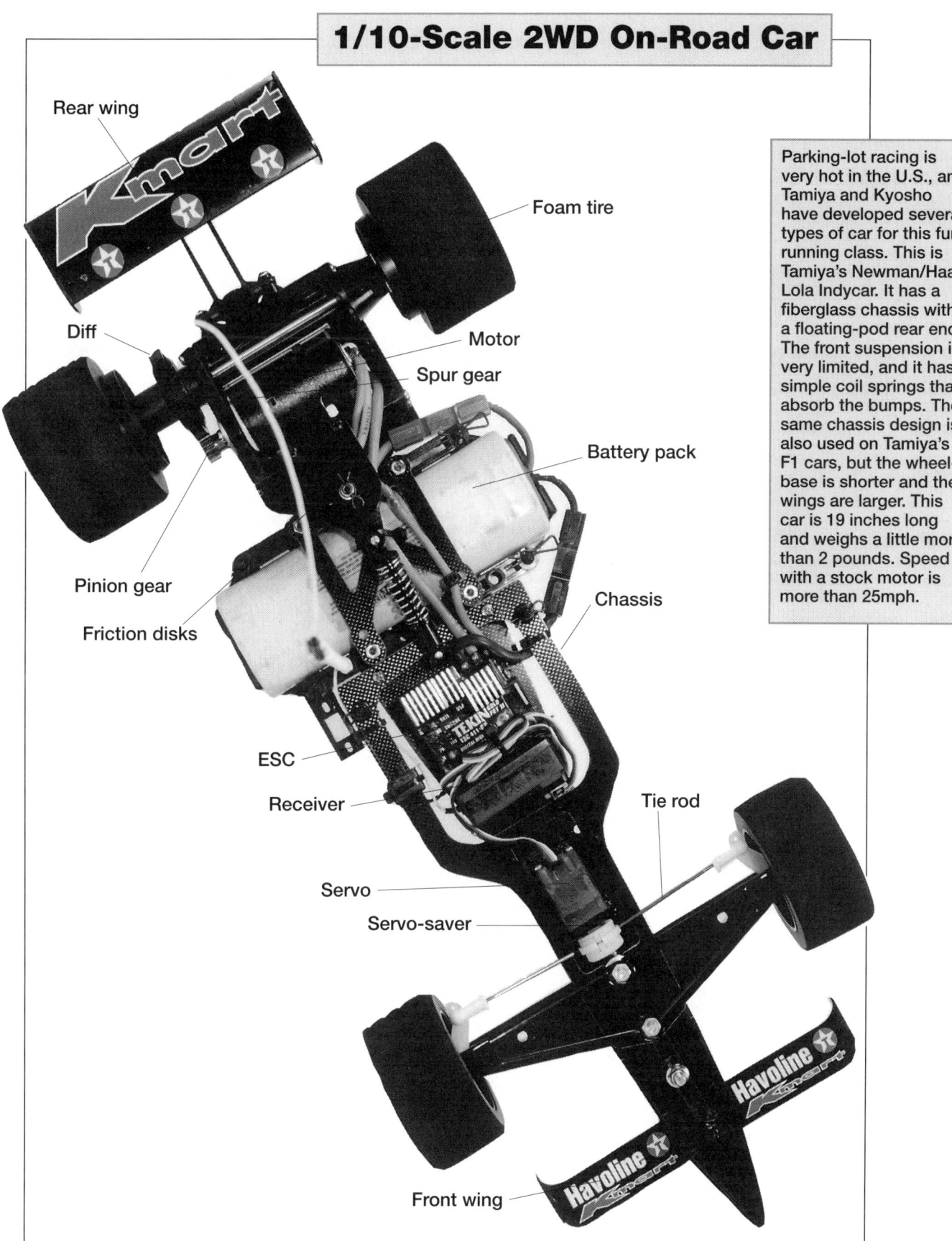

Parking-lot racing is very hot in the U.S., and Tamiya and Kyosho have developed several types of car for this fun-running class. This is Tamiya's Newman/Haas Lola Indycar. It has a fiberglass chassis with a floating-pod rear end. The front suspension is very limited, and it has simple coil springs that absorb the bumps. The same chassis design is also used on Tamiya's F1 cars, but the wheelbase is shorter and the wings are larger. This car is 19 inches long and weighs a little more than 2 pounds. Speed with a stock motor is more than 25mph.

1/12-Scale 2WD On-Road Pan Car

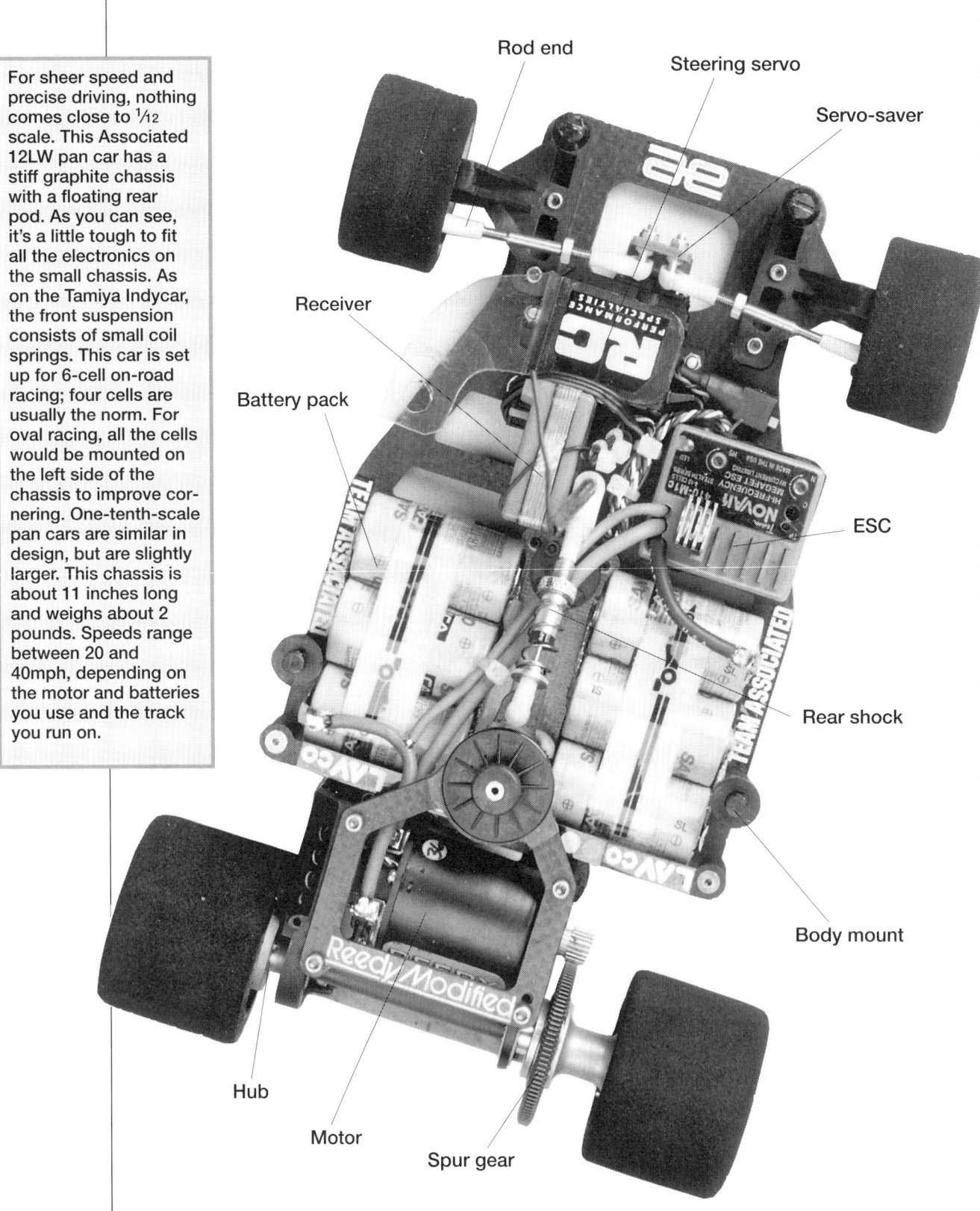

For sheer speed and precise driving, nothing comes close to 1/12 scale. This Associated 12LW pan car has a stiff graphite chassis with a floating rear pod. As you can see, it's a little tough to fit all the electronics on the small chassis. As on the Tamiya Indycar, the front suspension consists of small coil springs. This car is set up for 6-cell on-road racing; four cells are usually the norm. For oval racing, all the cells would be mounted on the left side of the chassis to improve cornering. One-tenth-scale pan cars are similar in design, but are slightly larger. This chassis is about 11 inches long and weighs about 2 pounds. Speeds range between 20 and 40mph, depending on the motor and batteries you use and the track you run on.

Labels: Rod end, Steering servo, Servo-saver, Receiver, Battery pack, ESC, Rear shock, Body mount, Hub, Motor, Spur gear

YOUR FIRST CAR

What You'll Need

If you're trying R/C cars for the first time, there a number of things you'll need. Of course, you'll need a car, but which kind? There are probably as many different kinds of R/C cars as there are full-size ones, so you have a lot to choose from. If you're an adult or an experienced model builder, you can basically choose any car you can afford. If you want a fast pavement screamer, look at electric pan cars. If you want to kick up some dirt in the backyard, go for an off-road buggy or truck. Gas-powered cars are faster, but they're a little trickier to run because they have small engines that need fine adjustments.

I recommend electric cars for beginners, because they're just plain easy to use. Charge 'em up, plug 'em in, and you're off! For a first car, stick to a 2-wheel-drive (2WD) car, because it will have fewer parts to deal with during assembly and maintenance. Two-wheel drive cars can be a little "skiddy" in the dirt, but this teaches you how to countersteer.

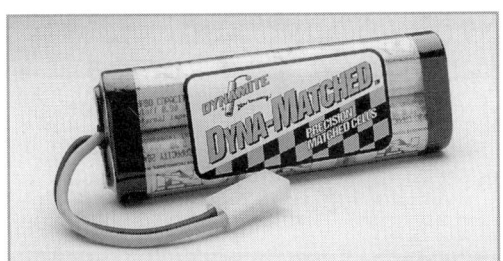

7.2V 6-cell stick pack.

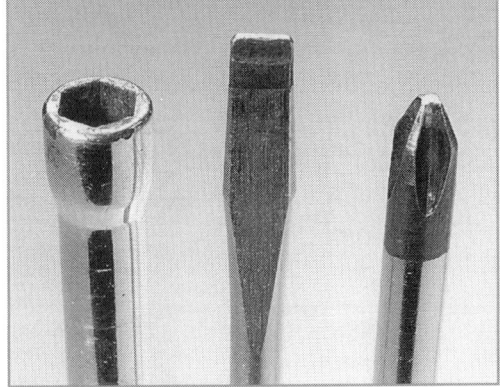

From left to right: nut driver, standard screwdriver and Phillips screwdriver.

You'll also need a radio system, a battery and a charger to complete your setup. Many shops offer a "combo" deal that completes any car kit they sell for less than $100. These are usually the best bets for beginners. Try to get a radio with servo-reversing and a power meter. I'll explain why you need these later, but do look for these features. Generally, the amount you spend on your car should determine how much you spend on your radio system. You don't want to run a $1,000 gas car with a $39 radio that has standard servos.

As far as tools are concerned, the more the better. Most car kits come with small Allen wrenches and nut drivers, but you'll also need a good assortment of both Phillips and standard screwdrivers. Always check to see whether your kit's parts are metric or standard. Generally, cars made in the USA, such as those from Associated* and Losi*, use standard threads, while cars from Asia, such as those from Tamiya* and Kyosho*, use metric threads. Make sure that the head of the screwdriver or the hex key fits the screws properly so you don't damage the screws. When you tighten a screw in a plastic part, make sure you don't strip out its threads. A self-tapping screw will cut threads as you screw it into the part, and if you force it after it has reached its maximum depth, it will strip the threads right out of the part.

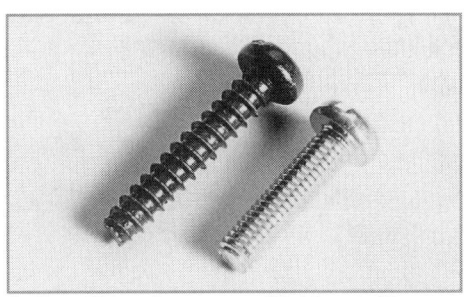

Left: self-tapping screw. Right: machine screw.

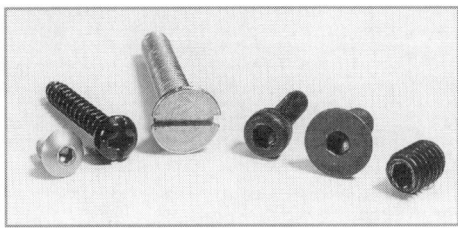

From left to right: button, Phillips, standard, hex-head, flat-head hex, setscrew.

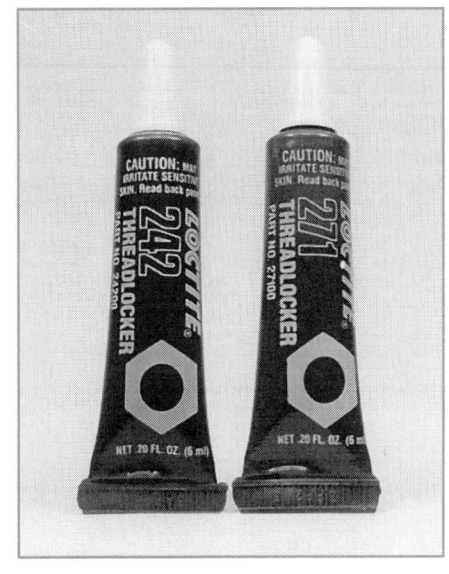

GETTING STARTED IN R/C CARS 13

CHAPTER 1

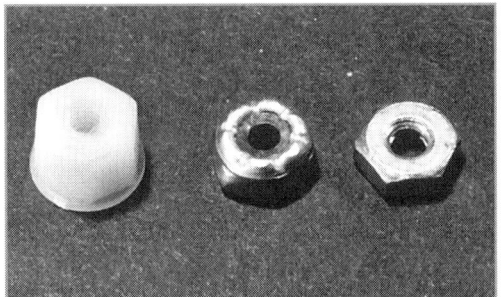

From left to right: nylon nut, locknut, plain nut.

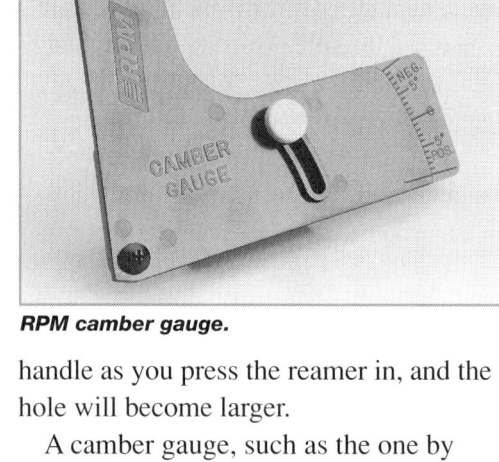

RPM camber gauge.

If you build a gas car, you must use threadlock! There's nothing worse than bringing your car in for fuel and finding that a whole bunch of parts are missing. Using threadlock when you build will save you time and money in the long run. Use the blue formula (no. 271) for metal nuts and bolts that you want to be able to take apart easily. For parts that you really want locked, like an engine flywheel, use the red formula (no. 272). This stuff is very strong and should not be used on tiny screws. If you put red threadlock on a small setscrew, you'll probably strip it trying to get it out. The heat of a torch will soften the strong stuff if you need to get it free again. Thread-lock isn't needed on screws that go into plastic or on locknuts that have nylon inserts because plastic and nylon parts grip the screws better than metal parts do.

Another tool you should have is *Radio Control Car Action*. Not only is every issue filled with articles about the hot new cars, but it also serves as a guide to tracks in your area, and it's a never-ending source of parts, kits and building tips.

Two other tools that make life easier are a tapered reamer and a camber gauge. With a tapered reamer, it's easy to make a perfectly round hole in your Lexan body for your mounts (or anything else). Twist the handle as you press the reamer in, and the hole will become larger.

A camber gauge, such as the one by RPM* shown here, will help you adjust all your linkages to the correct length. Just put the gauge on the ground and slide it against the side of the tire. By loosening the gauge's adjusting nut, you can adjust the gauge's angle from 10 degrees of positive camber to 10 degrees of negative camber. Then, you can simply adjust the tire's angle so it matches the angle of the gauge.

Hobby Shops and Mail Order Companies

Mail order companies and local hobby shops both have their good points and bad points. Prices are usually better through mail order, but who do you get to help you when your car doesn't work? Hobby shops have experienced employees who can help you with any problems you encounter. My advice for any beginner is to buy at a hobby shop. The little extra you'll pay will be more than offset by the help you'll get in the future. Call mail-order places only when you know exactly what you want and how to use it.

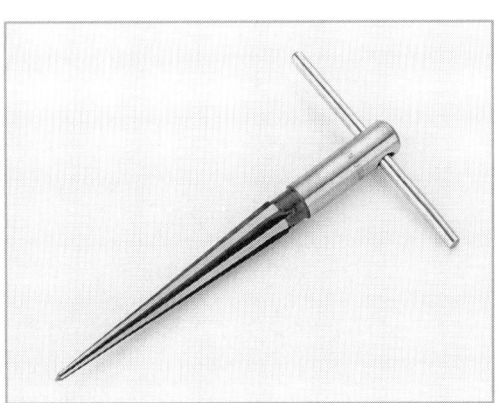

Dynamite tapered reamer.

CHAPTER 2

Electric Cars and Trucks

- 2WD and 4WD buggies

- Racing trucks

- Pan cars

- Parking-lot cars

- Specialty vehicles

CHAPTER 2

Many types of electric cars are available today, and each has a different design and purpose. Some are built for all-out speed, and others are meant for bashing around on dirt lots. Some are designed to be inexpensive, and others are designed to win races. If there's a track near you, see which classes of vehicle they run and choose a car that you can race there. And always, before you buy a new car, decide what you want from it.

OFF-ROAD

Two-Wheel-Drive Buggies

Because of their speed, handling and ease of operation, $\frac{1}{10}$-scale, two-wheel-drive (2WD), off-road buggies are very popular. Two-wheel-drive cars have a simple drive system and fewer moving parts than four-wheel-drive (4WD) cars, so maintenance is easier. Today, most 2WDs are very sophisticated and can handle rough terrain at high speeds. They're great for racing and for just bashing around. To handle the rough stuff, an off-road buggy needs a good suspension. Most have four-wheel (4W), independent suspensions with oil-filled shocks. Cars in this category include Associated's RC10; Losi's Junior 2, Pro SE and Double-X; Traxxas's* Rad 2, TRX-1 and TRX-3; Kyosho's Ultima and Outrage; Tamiya's Grasshopper 2, Bear Hawk, Dyna Storm and Super Hornet; and Schumacher's* Cougar and Cougar 2000.

Four-Wheel-Drive Buggies

Four-wheel-drive off-road cars are extremely nimble and can handle turns at higher speeds than 2WD cars can. Thanks to their powered front wheels, they don't fishtail as 2WD cars sometimes do. Power is delivered through a set of belts or drive shafts, and that makes the parts count a little higher, but the performance gain is worth the extra time spent building. As with the 2WD cars, these cars also have 4W independent suspensions with oil-filled shocks. These cars have front and rear gearboxes. For some reason, 4WD hasn't really caught on in the United States, but it's very popular in Europe and Asia. You can still find many tracks that have a 4WD class, but the turnout is usually much lower than it is for the 2WD class. Cars in this category are made by Yokomo*, Kyosho, Schumacher and Tamiya.

Racing Trucks

Racing trucks are almost as popular as buggies. It's no wonder: they evolved

ELECTRIC CARS AND TRUCKS

from 2WD buggies, so they have many of the same features and parts. For example, Associated's RC10 is also sold in a truck version called the RC10T. It uses the same chassis and gearbox, but it has longer arms and shocks and larger truck tires.

Team Losi was the first to produce a complete racing truck kit: the JRX-T. Now Team Associated offers the RC10T, Schumacher has the Nitro Storm 2000, Traxxas offers the SRT and MRC* has the MT-10S. Trucks are here to stay!

"Racing truck" doesn't mean that these vehicles are strictly for racing; they're just designed after stadium racing trucks—sort of. Racing trucks are a blast anywhere you drive them. They're just as fast as buggies, but with their larger tires, they're able to handle rougher ground. If you don't start out with a buggy, go for a racing truck!

ON-ROAD

Pan Cars—Oval

Pan cars have an unusual name, but because of their speed, they're worth checking out. The term "pan car" simply means that it has a flat chassis that's usually made of fiberglass or graphite. There are several types of pan-car racing

High-speed oval track.

in the U.S., but oval racing is probably the most popular form. Oval racing (which is similar to full-size NASCAR racing) is done either outdoors on a banked cement raceway or indoors on a carpet track. Either way, the cars are very fast.

Some tracks hold enduro races in which the cars have to pull into the pits for battery changes. There have even been races on a giant, banked, bicycle velodrome. Average speeds approach 50mph, and some cars have been clocked at more than 80mph!

Oval pan cars are sold in two scales—$1/10$ and $1/12$. They have the same fea-

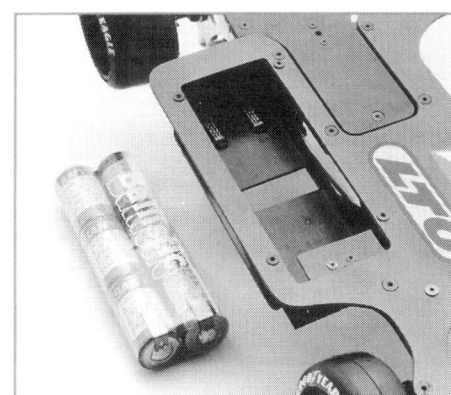

Bolink's quick-change battery system.

CHAPTER 2

TRC foam tires.

TRC rubber-capped tires.

An indoor, carpet, road-racing track.

tures (the $1/12$ cars are just smaller). Both scales use 6-cell battery packs, although the $1/12$-scales sometimes run with only a 4-cell pack. On an oval track, where the cars turn only to the left, racers often mount the batteries on the left side to help the car turn more efficiently and make the car faster and easier to handle.

In 1991, a new style of oval car hit the scene. Associated released a superspeedway version of the 10L called—of course—the 10LSS. (Superspeedway racing is a type of high-speed oval racing.) The 10LSS is considerably narrower than the standard 10L, and it looks more like a scale version of a full-size stock car. Another benefit of SS cars is that they have less frontal area, which means less resistance to the air. This makes the 10LSS faster than the old "wide cars." Soon after the introduction of the 10LSS, every major company—such as Bolink*, Cobra*, Corally*, Hyperdrive* and Trinity*—released an SS chassis.

When cars such as these run on carpet tracks, foam tires are the hot ticket. They do wear a little, but the traction is amazing. One major tire development is rubber-capped foam tires, which are made with the rubber found in full-size racing slicks. Made specifically for use on concrete and asphalt oval tracks, they don't have the

Wide pan & SS cars — ON-ROAD

Pan car — ON-ROAD

ELECTRIC CARS AND TRUCKS

greatest traction, cold, off the starting line, but when they're up to temperature and speed, they're far superior to plain foam. The rubber has much less rolling resistance than foam, so faster speeds are possible.

Pan Cars—Road

Another form of pan-car racing is road-course racing. Instead of following an oval, road racing is done on a flat, open area with plenty of right and left turns. On roadcourses, most of the cars have GTP bodies rather than oval stock-car bodies. Almost everything else about a road car is the same as an oval car, but the batteries are mounted on the chassis in a way that distributes the weight evenly.

Like oval racing, road racing can also be done inside, on carpet, with foam tires. Outside, these cars run on blacktop instead of concrete. Capped tires don't work on blacktop, so foam tires are used. To

Tamiya Mazda 787-B.

improve traction, many blacktop courses are sprayed down with sugar water or cola. This makes the surface tacky and prevents wheelspin.

Parking-Lot Cars

Many companies have developed cars that are designed for casual racing. This kind of racing is often called parking-lot racing because racers (a bunch of friends) simply lay out a simple course on the smoothest parking lot they can find.

Tamiya (Japan) is at the forefront of this movement with several classes of cars designed for parking-lot racing. One of the most popular is the Formula 1 (F1) class. These cars are similar to American-made pan cars, but they're less sophisticated. They're modeled after full-size cars on the

CHAPTER 2

Tamiya 190E EVO. II AMG.

Tamiya Ford Escort rally car.

F1 circuit, and they look extremely realistic. Kyosho also offers several F1 cars for parking-lot racing.

Because F1 racing isn't as popular in the States as it is in the rest of the world, Tamiya is now making Indycars. Their first version was the Newman/Haas Texaco Lola, modeled after the cars Nigel Mansell and Mario Andretti drove at the 1993 Indy 500. It's basically the same as the F1 chassis, but it's a bit longer and has smaller wings, like the full-size Indycars.

GTP race cars are my favorites. Tamiya and Kyosho make several models of GTP racers, such as the Nissan R91CP and the Mazda 787B. They, too, are similar to pan cars, but they're usually made of composite plastic and fiberglass rather than graphite.

Another very popular class in parking-lot racing is the sedan class. These cars are styled after racing versions of cars you might see on the street, such as Honda Civics and Alfa Romeo V55TIs. The sedan class is divided even further into cars with different applications. The Honda Civic is a front-wheel-drive model with treaded street tires. The Alfa is also for street racing, but it's 4WD, so it would have an advantage over the Honda. Another Tamiya model is the Ford Michelin Pilot Escort. It's designed after rally-cross racers that encounter several types of surface. Although its chassis is similar to the 4WD Alfa's, it has longer suspension travel and spiked tires for off- and on-road racing.

Dragsters

If speed is what you want and you want it quickly, check out an R/C dragster. These models will reach speeds of above 80mph in less than 3 seconds! A dragster is similar to a pan car, but it doesn't have a differential (diff) and its chassis has a very different shape. Just like the real thing, there are several types of R/C dragsters. One-tenth scale seems to be

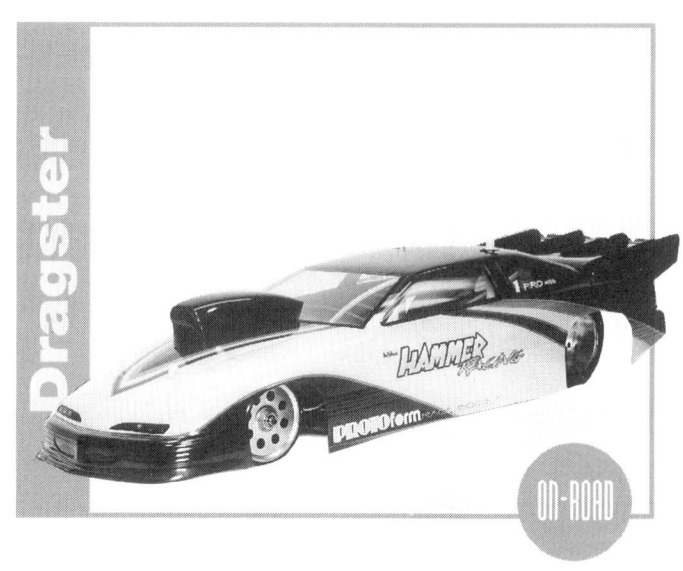

ELECTRIC CARS AND TRUCKS

more prevalent than 1/12 scale, although there are nitro-powered models as large as 1/6 to 1/4 scale (but this is a beginners' book, isn't it?!). There are rail chassis that are very long and thin, and funny-car and pro-stock chassis that are shorter and wider. Running hardware is usually the same: a microservo for steering and another one for a throttle switch; a receiver; and a motor.

Monster Trucks

Believe it or not, there are still more types of R/C vehicles. Monster trucks are very popular in full scale and in R/C. Tamiya introduced the first real monster—the Clod Buster—back in the late '80s. The Clod is a 4WD, 4WS, twin-motor giant crushing machine. It climbs steep hills, and it can even get over a downed telephone pole. Line up a few dozen empty soda cans and have a blast flatening them. The Clod has solid twin axles supported by four shocks. Kyosho also offers several monster trucks. Their cream of the crop is the USA-1, seen in full size at crushing events all over the country. It, too, is a twin-motor 4WD, 4WS truck, but it has a 4W independent suspension. Kyosho also has a gas version of their USA-1, and it has serious power!

Kyosho Hanging-On Racer motorcycle.

Specialty Vehicles

Some vehicles can't be put into a class. They range from two-wheel motorcycles to 18-wheel trucks. (I have yet to see an R/C unicycle!)

I've driven two R/C motorcycles and had a blast with each. The Royal* Hyperspeed bike is a large model—about 1/4 scale. It comes in two versions: assembled with the radio installed and in kit form. The best part about the Royal cycle is that it uses standard 6-cell battery

CHAPTER 2

Tamiya Globe Liner and Tanker Trailer.

packs and most R/C car motors. It's also pretty fast—about 22mph right out of the box. Like a real bike, it rides on only two wheels. When you turn the transmitter's wheel, the battery pack and the front fork shift to make the bike turn. Kyosho also offers a very cool motorcycle, but it's much smaller. It's $\frac{1}{8}$ scale and very detailed, and, get this: the driver moves from side to side as the bike leans. Even though it's smaller, it has some nice performance features, such as a real chain-drive system and oil-filled shocks.

Taking a jump from two to 18 wheels, I must mention the $\frac{1}{14}$-scale Tamiya big rigs. There are two such models in Tamiya's lineup: a flat-nose cab-over type and a conventional Kenworth model. They both have plastic and aluminum chassis, a three-speed transmission and eight driven wheels. But Tamiya didn't stop with the cabs—no way! They also offer an aluminum refrigerator trailer and a stainless-steel tanker trailer. Attach one of them to a cab, and you have a huge rig that's more than 3 feet long!

As you can see, there are many types of cars to choose from—some aren't even cars at all!—and I haven't mentioned gas-powered vehicles yet. Always consider what you want from your vehicle, and make your choice accordingly.

CHAPTER 3

Electric Motors and Gearing

- Motor makeup

- Brushes

- Springs

- Gear ratios

- Motor maintenance

CHAPTER 3

Electric motors are made up of several intricate components. Look at the diagram below while you read this to help you understand where the parts are.

• The motor's housing is called the can. It's made of steel and has a bearing or bushing in the center of one end. Two semicircular magnets are mounted exactly 180 degrees apart on the inside wall of the can.

• The moving component in a motor is a shaft that's called the armature (or "arm" for short). It has three sections of metal laminations (called poles) attached to its middle. Copper wire is wrapped around each of the three poles and is attached to the top of the armature at the commutator (or comm), which is a round copper section above the poles that's divided into three segments. The arm is inserted into the motor can with the shaft exiting through the bearing in the end. Very little space is left between the magnets and the armature, but that's necessary for proper operation.

• The other end of the armature is supported by the endbell—a bearing in a plastic or aluminum housing. It's screwed onto the open end of the can to form a complete unit.

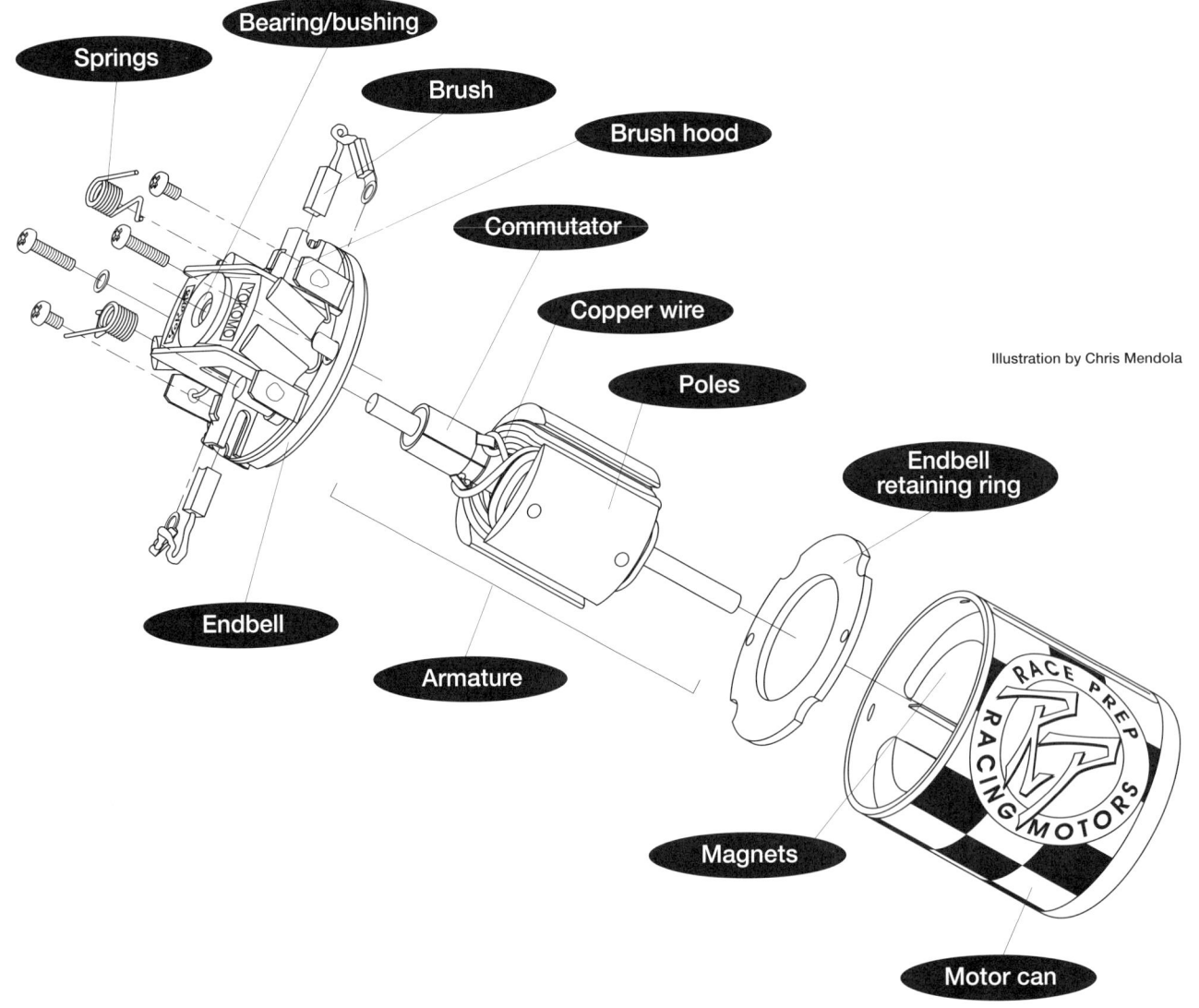

Illustration by Chris Mendola

ELECTRIC MOTORS AND GEARING

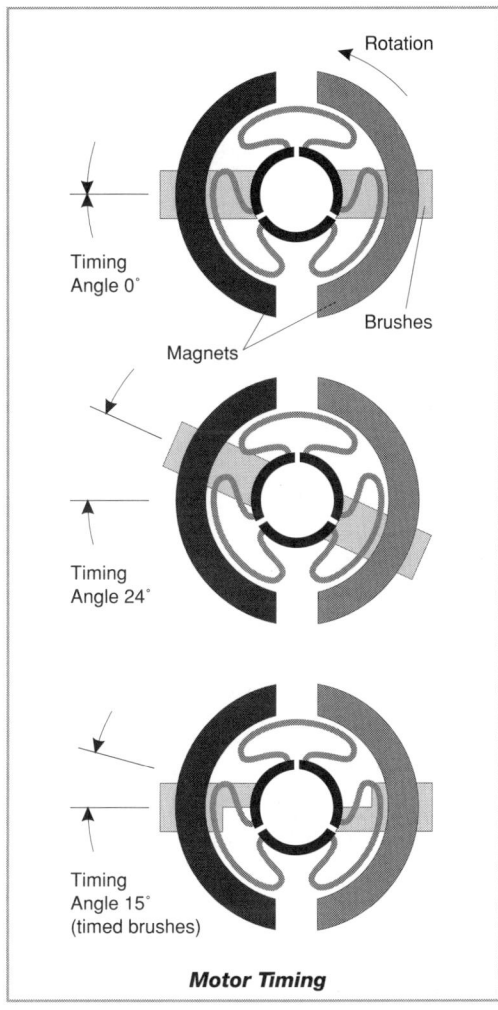
Motor Timing

continue to spin.
• The position of the brushes in relation to the motor magnets is called timing (see diagram, left). When the brushes are centered on the magnets, you have zero degrees of timing. You can adjust timing by about 10 degrees in either direction, but that's about it. Timing changes will affect your run time, torque and speed. A good rule is not to mess with timing until you have the equipment to measure the changes you make.

What's the Difference?
The main thing that sets motors apart is how the armature has been made. Different gauges (size) and number of turns of wire can be wound around the arm to achieve different results. For example, a 14-turn quad motor is made up of four strands of wire wrapped around each pole of the arm 14 times. A 10-turn single is made up of a single strand of wire wrapped around the arm 10 times. Generally speaking, the fewer the turns, the faster the motor. To figure out which motor is right for your

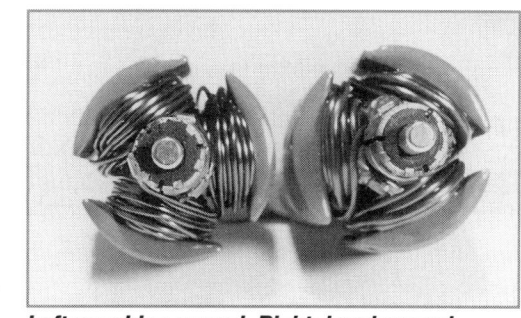
Left: machine-wound. Right: hand-wound.

• On either side of the endbell are two metal housings called brush hoods. They hold the motor brushes exactly 180 degrees apart. The brushes are inserted into the hoods and contact the commutator. Two small springs hold the brushes firmly against the comm.
• When voltage is applied to the two motor brushes, the wire on the armature takes on a different magnetic state. The difference between the magnetic field of the can and the arm causes the armature to rotate within the can. As the armature turns, the brushes contact different sections of the commutator, changing the magnetic state of the arm again. This causes the motor to continue rotating. As long as voltage is supplied to the motor, the armature will

The gauge of wire and the number of wraps around the armature determine a motor's performance.

CHAPTER 3

Which motor is best?

Car	Turns										
	17	16	15	14	13	12	11	10	9	8	7
1/10 on-road—4 min.	–	–	–	–	■	■	■	■	–	–	–
1/10 oval—4 min.	–	–	■	■	■	■	■	■	–	–	–
1/12 on-road—8 min.; 6-cell	■	■	■	■	–	–	–	–	–	–	–
1/12 oval—5 min.; 6-cell	–	–	■	■	■	■	–	–	–	–	–
1/12 carpet—8 min.; 4-cell	–	–	■	■	■	■	■	–	–	–	–
1/10 off-road—4 min.; 6-cell	–	■	■	■	■	■	■	■	–	–	–
1/10 truck—4 min.; 6-cell	■	■	■	■	■	■	–	–	–	–	–
4WD dirt oval—4 min.; 7-cell	–	–	–	■	■	■	■	■	–	–	–
2WD dirt oval—4 min.; 7-cell	–	–	■	■	■	■	■	–	–	–	–
1/10 sprint car—4 min.; 7-cell	–	–	–	■	■	■	–	–	–	–	–
Drag racing	–	–	–	–	–	–	■	■	■	■	■
Truck pulling	–	–	–	–	–	■	■	■	■	■	–

application, see the chart above.

Another difference between motors is the way in which the armature has been wound. On some motors, the wire is wound by hand; hence the description "hand-wound." Some armatures are wound by machine...and yes, they're called "machine-wound." So what's the difference? The most obvious difference is the price. It simply takes longer to wind wire by hand, so hand-wound motors are more expensive. The real difference, however, is the quality. When wound by hand, the wires are wrapped with care, and the result is more uniform and neat. Machine-wound motors generally look sloppier. On the track, the difference may not be as apparent at first. Both winding methods work well and produce fast motors. But under serious load, a poorly wound armature can sometimes detonate, or "throw a wind." This is when a loop of wire comes free and starts to hit the magnets. If the wire doesn't jam the motor right away, the motor usually overheats and becomes a big smoke bomb.

Brushes

When I first heard of a motor brush, I was expecting to see something with bristles

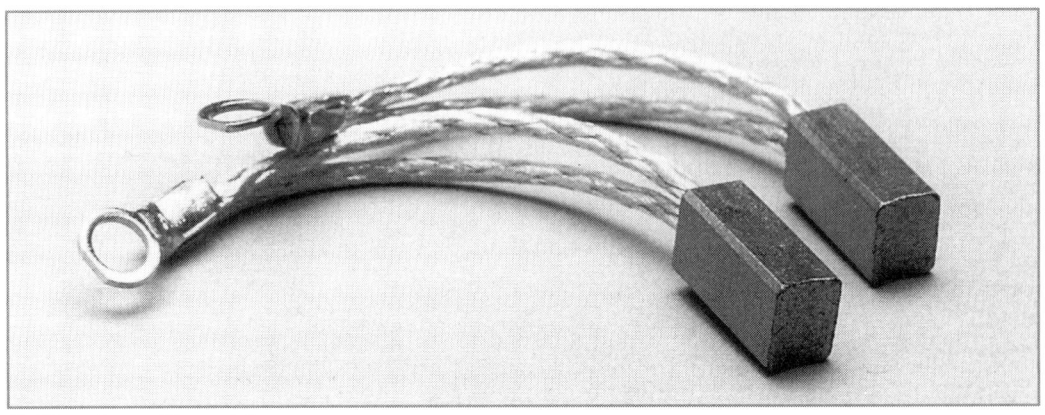

Full brushes with eyelets.

ELECTRIC MOTORS AND GEARING

Several examples of cut and full brushes.

on it, but that's not the case. A motor brush has no bristles and looks nothing like a toothbrush or a hair brush. In fact, it looks like a chunk of copper with a wire on it, but I guess they couldn't just call it that.

A motor brush is actually a mixture of several metals (including copper and silver) and lubricants. They carry the current from your battery to the rotating commutator. The power your motor can put out depends in large part on the brush's shape (or cut) and composition, and the pressure of the brush against the comm.

Brushes are sold in a vast array of styles. A full-size brush fits exactly into the brush hood and is basically rectangular. If you reduce the part of the brush that contacts the commutator, you can change the motor's punch (and several other properties). These brushes are called "cut," and, as you might expect, there are several different ways to cut a brush.

In stock racing, cut brushes are commonly called timed brushes, because a stock motor has fixed timing. A timed brush is cut vertically so that half of the brush's face is removed. Cutting a brush in this way advances the timing slightly for more speed on the track.

Off-road brushes are also cut to remove half of the surface that touches the comm, but they're cut horizontally rather than vertically. With this type of brush, timing isn't affected, and less of the comm is worn. Several other cuts are also available but, hey, this is a beginners' book, isn't it?!

Brushes should be replaced after every couple of runs in racing, but for general use, they should be changed when they're worn down so much that they're too short for the springs to hold them against the comm properly. Try to replace them with the same kind.

Springs

A small spring holds each motor brush firmly against the comm. As with most things in R/C, there are several types of springs. Basically, light springs don't put a lot of tension on the brushes, and heavy

Off-road cut brushes.

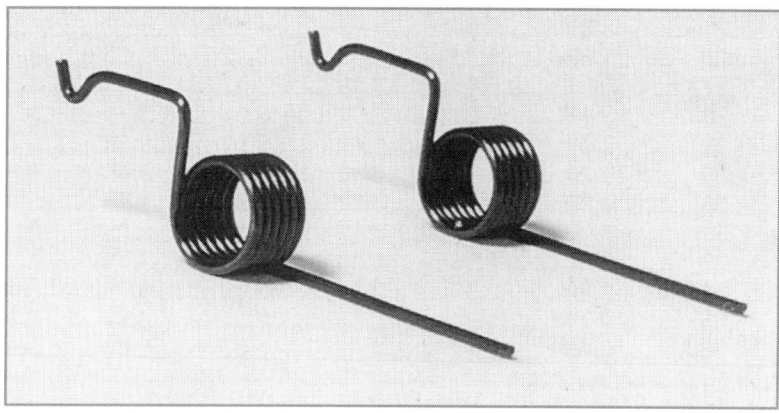

Motor brush springs.

GEAR RATIOS

48-Pitch

Gear	72	75	78	81	82	84	86
12	6.00	6.25	6.50	6.75	6.83	7.00	7.16
13	5.53	5.77	6.00	6.23	6.30	6.46	6.61
14	5.14	5.35	5.57	5.78	5.85	6.00	6.14
15	4.80	5.00	5.20	5.40	5.46	5.60	5.73
16	4.50	4.68	4.87	5.06	5.12	5.25	5.37
17	4.23	4.41	4.58	4.76	4.82	4.94	5.05
18	4.00	4.16	4.33	4.50	4.55	4.66	4.77
19	3.79	3.94	4.10	4.26	4.31	4.42	4.52
20	3.60	3.75	3.90	4.05	4.10	4.20	4.30
21	3.42	3.57	3.71	3.85	3.90	4.00	4.09
22	3.27	3.41	3.54	3.68	3.72	3.81	3.90
23	3.13	3.26	3.39	3.52	3.56	3.65	3.74
24	3.00	3.12	3.25	3.37	3.41	3.50	3.58
25	2.88	3.00	3.12	3.24	3.28	3.36	3.44
26	2.77	2.88	3.00	3.11	3.15	3.23	3.30
27	2.66	2.77	2.88	3.00	3.03	3.11	3.18
28	2.57	2.67	2.78	2.89	2.92	3.00	3.07
29	2.48	2.58	2.68	2.79	2.82	2.89	2.96
30	2.40	2.50	2.60	2.70	2.73	2.80	2.86

64-Pitch

Gear	96	98	100	102	104	106	108	110	115	120
18	5.33	5.44	5.55	5.66	5.77	5.88	6.00	6.11	6.38	6.66
19	5.05	5.15	5.26	5.36	5.47	5.57	5.68	5.79	6.05	6.31
20	4.80	4.90	5.00	5.10	5.20	5.30	5.40	5.50	5.75	6.00
21	4.57	4.66	4.76	4.85	4.95	5.04	5.14	5.23	5.47	5.71
22	4.36	4.45	4.54	4.63	4.72	4.81	4.90	5.00	5.22	5.45
23	4.17	4.26	4.34	4.43	4.52	4.60	4.69	4.78	5.00	5.21
24	4.00	4.08	4.16	4.25	4.33	4.41	4.50	4.58	4.79	5.00
25	3.84	3.92	4.00	4.08	4.16	4.24	4.32	4.40	4.60	4.80
26	3.69	3.76	3.84	3.92	4.00	4.07	4.15	4.23	4.42	4.61
27	3.55	3.63	3.70	3.77	3.85	3.92	4.00	4.07	4.26	4.44
28	3.43	3.50	3.57	3.64	3.71	3.78	3.85	3.92	4.10	4.28
29	3.31	3.38	3.44	3.51	3.58	3.65	3.72	3.79	3.96	4.13
30	3.20	3.26	3.33	3.40	3.46	3.53	3.60	3.66	3.83	4.00
31	3.09	3.16	3.22	3.29	3.35	3.42	3.48	3.54	3.71	3.87
32	3.00	3.06	3.12	3.18	3.25	3.31	3.37	3.43	3.59	3.75
33	2.90	2.96	3.03	3.09	3.15	3.21	3.27	3.33	3.48	3.63
34	2.82	2.88	2.94	3.00	3.05	3.11	3.17	3.23	3.38	3.52
35	2.74	2.80	2.85	2.91	2.97	3.02	3.08	3.14	3.28	3.42
36	2.66	2.72	2.77	2.83	2.88	2.94	3.00	3.05	3.19	3.33

ones do. Always try to use replacement brushes that are the same as, or close to, the original ones. I don't want to confuse you with too many choices, so just stick with the brushes and springs that were designed for your motor.

Gear Ratios

A car's gear ratio is very important. It determines how many times the wheels turn with every rotation of the motor. This ratio will have a great effect on the car's acceleration and top speed. Selecting the right ratio is just as important as it is when you ride a 10-speed bike. Using a very low gear ratio is like trying to ride a bike up a hill in 10th gear.

To figure out what your gear ratio is, take the number of teeth on the larger gear (spur), and divide it by the number of teeth on the smaller one (pinion). Let's say you have a pan car, such as the Associated RC10L. With an 80-tooth spur gear and a 15-tooth pinion, your ratio would be 5.33 to 1 (80 ÷ 15 = 5.33). That means that the motor turns 5.33 times for every revolution of the wheels. By increasing the number of teeth on the pinion, you'll decrease the ratio and increase top speed. Using a smaller spur gear has the same effect.

Decreasing the pinion size reduces top speed, but increases the acceleration and run time. Because most races in the States

Spur (larger) and pinion (smaller) gears.

are 4 minutes long, racers must gear to achieve maximum speed without exhausting the batteries in less than 4 minutes. They also don't want too much juice left at the end of a race; it could have been used for more speed. Besides the gear ratio, motor selection and battery type play a major role in speed and duration.

It's easy to figure out the gear ratio of a direct-drive car like the 10L I mentioned before, but what about a car with a gearbox? A gearbox just adds another step to the equation, because it involves an additional set of gears and another ratio. Let's say you have an RC10 buggy with the Stealth transmission. First, you have a similar spur and pinion setup. (Let's say we have the same size gears on this car: an 80-tooth spur and a 15-tooth pinion for a ratio of 5.33 to 1.) The tranny has a fixed ratio of 2.25 to 1. To get the total transmission ratio, multiply the gearbox ratio by the primary ratio (2.25 x 5.33 = 11.99 to 1). This means that the motor turns over 11.99 times for every wheel revolution. The key to understanding gear ratios is experimentation. Try a selection of ratios until you find the perfect balance of speed, acceleration and run time.

CHAPTER 3

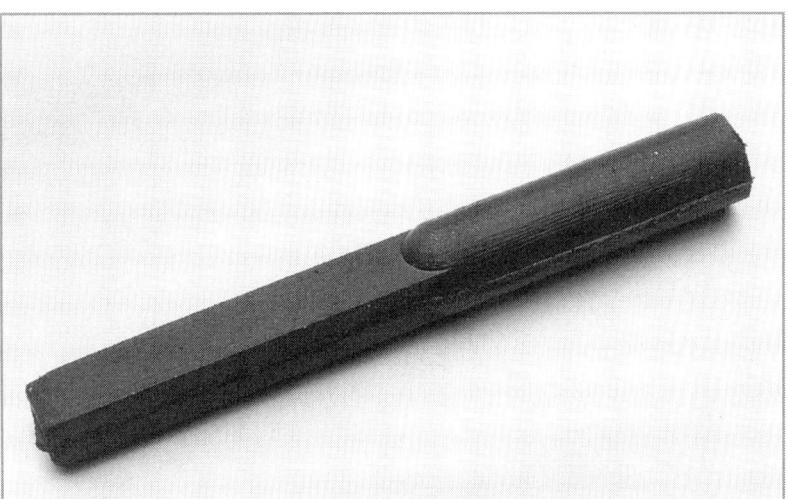

Commutator cleaning stick.

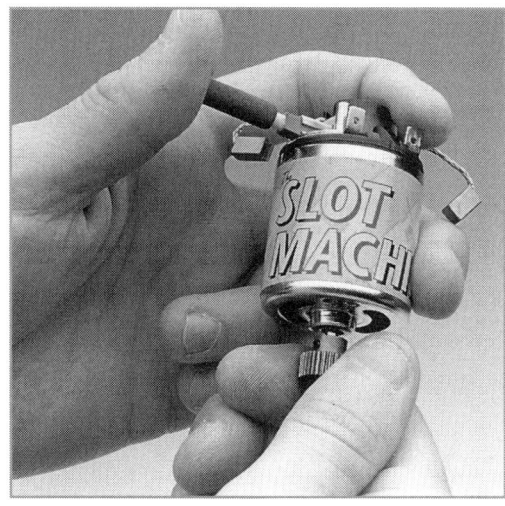

To polish the comm, insert a comm stick into the brush hoods and turn the armature.

Motor Maintenance

When you run a motor, the brushes constantly feed power to the comm. As the brushes switch between the different segments of the comm, small sparks are generated; this is known as arcing, and it will eventually wear the brushes and the commutator. A glazed coating forms on the brushes; this restricts power and makes the motor inefficient. The comm develops tiny pits and a black carbon buildup. After a while, if the brushes and comm aren't cared for, "dead" spots will form on the motor. A dead spot on the comm won't conduct electricity. Your car might run, but if it stops when the motor is in a certain position, the motor might not start turning again. A slight bump might get the car going again, but the motor is really in need of attention.

To polish the comm between runs, insert a device called a comm stick into one of the brush slots. Comm sticks are usually made of a rubber-like material that's impregnated with a light abrasive and, when used properly, they won't damage the comm. Only a slight amount of pressure (while you turn the comm) is needed to get the comm looking good again. You can also clean brushes with a comm stick, but if there's any question about whether they're shot, replace them.

Even with maintenance, the comm will show signs of wear. When the comm is beyond the help of a comm stick, it must be re-cut. Cutting is removing a thin layer of the comm's surface with a lathe. Some lathes are available at hobby shops, but they're too expensive for beginners. Check to see whether a hobby shop in your area will cut your comm for you, or send it back to the manufacturer. After the comm has been cut, the motor will perform like new again. After cutting a comm, always use new brushes.

A comm lathe will bring a worn comm back to life.

ELECTRIC MOTORS AND GEARING

Cleaning

It's a good idea to spray your motor with motor cleaner after every few runs—outside, or in a place with good ventilation. If you have a stock motor with bushings, simply remove the brushes and spray the motor out. Always add a drop of light oil to each bushing after cleaning.

A modified motor with bearings will need slightly different care, because spraying will force dirt into the bearings. When I clean a modified motor, I like to take it apart completely. First, remove the brushes and springs, then mark the can. Because the orientation of the can and endbell set the timing, you want to be able to put the motor back together in the original way. Now loosen the two screws on the endbell, but don't remove them. After loosening the screws, you should be able to twist the endbell. Turn it slowly while pulling it up gently; the endbell will simply lift off. To catch any shims on the shaft, remove the endbell over a towel; if there are any shims, be sure to set them aside. A shim might also stick to the bearing. Remember, you want to put the motor back together

To remove the endbell, loosen the two endbell screws.

as it was originally, so if there are four shims on the top end of the shaft, put four back on.

Now you can remove the armature. It's difficult to remove because the magnets in the can hold it in place. Pull it out gently, noting whether there are any shims. They might stick on the bearing, or on a magnet. Now you can begin to clean the motor.

Start by spraying the armature with motor cleaner. Black fluid will stream from the motor wire as the carbon and dirt are

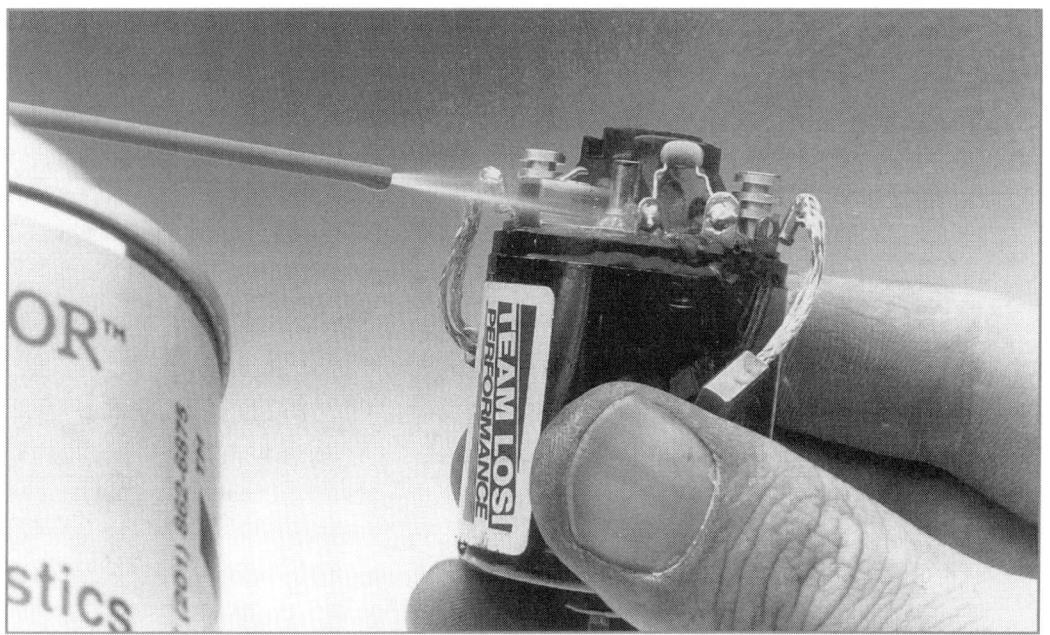
Motor spray will remove the carbon and dirt that can accumulate in a motor.

CHAPTER 3

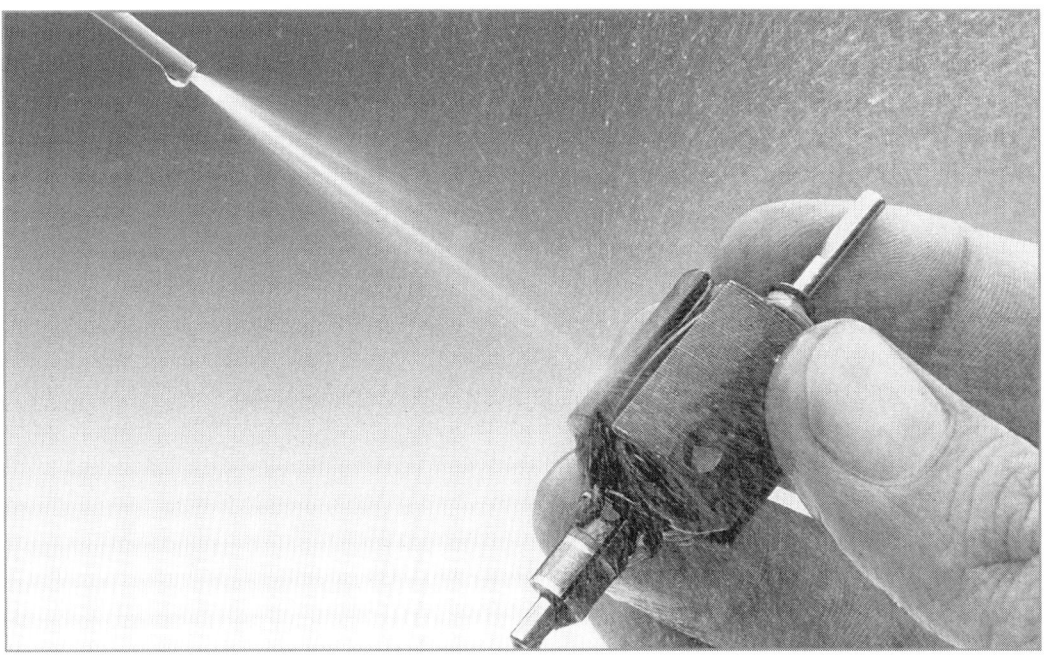

removed. When the fluid runs clean, set the armature aside to dry. Then start cleaning the endbell. Spray it from all sides and be sure to get the bearing. Slide the bearing over an end of the armature shaft and give it a spin. It should spin freely and smoothly; gritty is bad! You can spray the bearing while it's on the armature, spinning it to remove all the dirt. Set it aside to dry. Do the same for the can and check its bearing, too. When everything is clean and dry, add a drop of light oil to each bearing and let it soak in.

Next, you can start to rebuild the motor. Add the shims to the armature on the pinion-gear end, and slide the armature into the can. Be careful, because the can will be pulling the armature in. Make sure you get the shaft through the bearing. Add the other shims to the other end of the arm, and put the endbell back on the can. Align the bearings with the shaft and press lightly. To get the endbell locked on again, press lightly on the screw heads while turning the endbell. Once again, the endbell will snap onto the can. Rotate the endbell so that it is as it was before the rebuild.

Now that you know which components make up a motor, which components can vary in motors (this can make a big difference to performance) and how to properly care for your motor, you'll be able to keep it running strong.

When you rebuild a motor, be sure to put the shims back on as they were before the rebuild.

CHAPTER 4

R/C Electronics

- Radio features

- AM, FM and PCM

- Speed controls

- Crystals

- Servos and receivers

CHAPTER 4

Your radio system gives you control of your vehicle. It's the "R" in "R/C" (no, it doesn't stand for "remote"!). Systems vary from a simple 2-stick transmitter that costs less than $50 to complex wheel types that can cost as much as $300. I'll try to explain how a radio system operates—without making your head spin.

The transmitter is the part you hold in your hands. When you move a control on the transmitter with your hand, the movement is turned into a coded signal. This signal is sent to the receiver by radio waves. The receiver, which is mounted in the car, gets the signal and passes it along to a servo that reproduces the mechanical movement. Most radios have two channels of control: one for steering and one for throttle.

A stick radio has two joysticks for control. One moves from left to right to control steering, and one moves forward or backward to control direction and speed. A pistol-grip radio has a wheel to control direction and a trigger to control throttle and brakes.

All radios are what is called "digital proportional." This simply means that the movement you make on the transmitter is proportional to the movement of the servo in the car.

R/C ELECTRONICS

Some radios use trim dials; some, such as the radio above, use push-buttons.

Dual-rate dials on pistol-grip radios are positioned so that you can adjust them with your thumb.

Radios are set apart by their features and adjustments. For example, if you turn your control to the left but your car turns to the right, you need to reverse something to get things going in the right direction. You can reverse the mechanical linkage in the car, or, with some radios, you can flip a reversing switch on the transmitter. The more expensive radios offer even more adjustments.

All transmitters have trim-adjustment dials. With these dials, you can make minor adjustments to the neutral position of your car's two channels. One dial is used to make the car track straight when you let go of the wheel/stick; the other determines the neutral setting for the throttle trigger/stick. These dials are always positioned so that you can adjust them while you drive.

More Advanced Features

Some radios offer a multitude of transmitter adjustments. The controls range from tiny trim potentiometers to computer-controlled menus.

• **Dual rate**. Dual rate (D/R) is a steering adjustment that affects the amount of travel a servo will reproduce. Turning the dial to 10 causes the front wheels to turn to their maximum—say, 30 degrees from straight. If you reduce the D/R number to 5, the wheels will turn only to 15 degrees in each direction. The distance you turn the transmitter's wheel remains the same. With a pistol-grip radio, you can easily adjust D/R with your thumb while you drive.

• **Endpoint adjust, adjustable travel volume (EPA, ATV).** Like D/R, EPA is used to set how far a servo can turn. This control, however, is a small potentiometer on a control panel of the transmitter, and it was designed only for setting up a system before you drive the car. Set the endpoints to turn the wheels as far as they can go. Make sure the D/R dial is set to maximum before you set the steering endpoints, so you will still be able to adjust D/R as you drive. EPA is used for both steering and throttle.

• **Sub-trim.** Some radios have a control called sub-trim, which is another trim potentiometer. It's also used to adjust the neutral setting of the servos, but because it's on a control panel, it's used only during setup. Center the main trim dials, and then adjust the sub-trim to set the servos at neutral. You can make small adjustments later with the main trim dials.

CHAPTER 4

Endpoint adjust (EPA, ATV) | Exponential (EXP) | Sub-Trim

Signal comparison
- AM (Amplitude Modulation)
- FM (Frequency Modulation)
- PCM 1024 (High Resolution)

- **Exponential (EXP).** Exponential is a very useful feature that many people don't understand. I said before that your servo moves in direct proportion to the amount you turn your wheel. Well, think of exponential as a way to alter the proportions of your control. In some instances, your car might be very sensitive to steering at high speeds; you give it the slightest bit of steering, and it veers sharply to the left or right. With a little exponential, you can desensitize the steering near neutral and gain more control. But the great part about EXP is that it doesn't affect the total amount of servo travel. With EXP, you can make the car easier to drive straight, and you can still use full steering when conditions call for it.

AM, FM and PCM

There are basically three types of radio-signal transmission. Without getting into the scientific explanation of what AM (amplitude modulation) is, I'll simply say it's the simplest, least expensive method of signal transmission. The next type is FM (frequency modulation). FM has slightly better range and is less susceptible to radio interference. It's also a little more expensive. The last type is PCM (pulse-code modulation). PCM is a type of AM or FM modulation, but it has greater range and resolution. PCM signals are coded in such a way that interference is almost nonexistent. Most PCM radios also have a feature that will return the servos to a pre-set location, e.g., full brakes in the event of interference. In general, the amount you pay for your car should determine the type of radio you use. Don't buy a $300 PCM radio for a $75 car, or try to run a $1,000 gas car with a $45 AM radio.

R/C ELECTRONICS

Servos

One of the most important components of any R/C car is the servo. The servo reproduces your movements to guide your model. Most radio systems come with "standard" servos, such as the Futaba* S148 or the JR* NES-507. Standard servos are inexpensive and will work well with most entry-level vehicles, but they aren't suitable for larger vehicles.

What sets servos apart is their power and speed. A standard S-148 servo has a speed of 0.22 second for its 60 degrees of travel. Power is measured in ounce-inches of torque (the S148 has 42 oz.-in). Although this is OK for most cars, others need servos that offer more power.

For an on-road car, you don't need a servo with lots of torque, you need a quick servo that will help you make rapid, tight turns. A Futaba S132H has a speed of 0.13 second and 25 oz.-in. of torque, which is perfect for this type of application.

Gas cars and monster trucks need lots of torque to turn their tires and jam their brakes. For these vehicles, there are even more serious servos; for example, the Futaba S9302 has a speed of 0.19 second with—get this—99 oz.-in. of torque! And,

Futaba's heavy-duty S-9302.

as if that wasn't enough, the servo's gears are heavy-duty brass instead of plastic.

Many other servos have even more impressive specifications, but this should give you an idea of what's available. And remember, just because you have a Futaba radio system, it doesn't mean that you have to use a Futaba servo. Many times, I've run my Futaba radio system with a KO* steering servo and an Airtronics* throttle servo. The only thing you must do to use other servos is to check the connections. All servos have three wires that connect them to receivers. One is for positive power, one is for negative, and the third is for the radio signal. As nice as it is that all servos have the same three wires, they aren't always in the same order or in the same colors. See the sidebar "Servos and Receivers" in this chapter for information on how to convert servos to different radio systems.

Speed Controls

Just as the name implies, a speed control governs your car's speed. There are two methods by which this can be achieved. The simplest and cheapest type of speed control is mechanical. It's basically a

A standard Futaba S-148.

CHAPTER 4

three-step (low, medium and high) switch and a resistor. A servo is used to flip the switch from low to medium to full blast, and usually two or three speeds in reverse.

Some mechanical speed controls use a variable resistor to provide a wider range of speed choices. Although mechanical speed controls work well, they have some drawbacks. First, they're not very efficient. When you drive at any speed other than full, a resistor limits the amount of power that's delivered to your motor, and energy is wasted in the form of heat. The constant movement of the switch causes arcing that eventually wears dead spots into the speed control. The carbon buildup can, however, be cleaned away with fine sandpaper. Always use the kit's switch lube if the instructions call for it.

Electronic speed controls (ESCs) are the wave of the future. Without any moving parts, they control the power delivery to your motor and provide an almost "stepless" (no low-medium-high) output of power to your commands. Field-effect transistors (also known as FETs) regulate the power in rapid pulses. Because there aren't any moving parts or servo transit times to deal with, an ESC can deliver full power as fast as you can jam on the throttle. And not only are they efficient, but most new models also recover some of the power used for braking and deliver it back to the battery!

As sophisticated as they sound, most ESCs are easy to set up. After you've hooked it up to the receiver (with the correct connector, of course) you simply adjust two small trim-potentiometers with a little screwdriver. Most ESCs have a light to help make setup easier. Turn the neutral dial until the light goes out, and check it by hooking up a motor. If the ESC is in neutral, the motor will be silent. Give the trigger a little pull and see if the motor starts to turn. If it doesn't, you might have to reverse the channel. Check this by flicking the trigger in the opposite direction. If the motor turns, then reverse channel two on your transmitter. Now pull the trigger as far as it will go. Depending on the

A mechanical speed control uses a resistor to provide three levels of speed.

Novak's One-Touch ESC, the Rooster.

R/C ELECTRONICS

Tekin's 411-G2 uses trim pots to adjust neutral and full speed.

manufacturer, at full throttle, the light should come on or go out. Adjust the second ESC dial so that the speed maxes out just before the trigger hits the end of its travel. The ESC's light and the sound of the motor will let you know you're at full speed.

Every manufacturer uses its own methods for setup, so read the instructions! Some very high-tech features have begun to show up in ESCs. Novak*, Tekin* and SCI* have done away with the dials and have replaced them with a single push-button. All you have to do is turn your system on, push the setup button on the ESC, pull the throttle trigger first to full speed, then to neutral and then to brake. That's it! The settings are stored in the ESC until you change them, even if you disconnect the battery.

Crystals

Every radio system needs crystals to operate. The crystals determine which channel the radio operates on in one of the available bands. Crystals are used in a pair: one for the transmitter and one for the receiver. If you try to run with a friend and you're both on the same channel, one of you will have to change crystals, or you won't both

1991 LEGAL FREQUENCIES

26MHz and 27MHz —aircraft, cars and boats

Frequency	Flag color (USA)
26.995	Brown
27.045	Red
27.095	Orange
27.145	Yellow
27.195	Green
27.255	Blue

75MHz—cars and boats

Frequency	Channel no.
75.410	61
75.430	62
75.450	63
75.470	64
75.490	65
75.510	66
75.530	67
75.550	68
75.570	69
75.590	70
75.610	71
75.630	72
75.650	73
75.670	74
75.690	75
75.710	76
75.730	77
75.750	78
75.770	79
75.790	80
75.810	81
75.830	82
75.850	83
75.870	84
75.890	85
75.910	86
75.930	87
75.950	88
75.970	89
75.990	90

be able to control your cars.

In the USA, we're restricted to two bands—75MHz and 27MHz. Within those bands, there are more than 20 channels (frequencies) from which to choose. Most racers recommend that you don't switch from a channel that's too far from the one

CHAPTER 4

Servos and Receivers

All receivers have the same three-wire setup for connecting servos, but each servo has a different plastic housing and its own order for its wires. You can adapt any servo to work with any receiver as long as you swap the wires correctly. Here's a list of servo connectors and receivers and their polarities.

Every receiver has a row of jacks in which to plug servos, a receiver battery, or an ESC. Each jack has three pins: one is for positive power, one is for negative, and the other is for the signal that controls the servo and/or ESC. As a rule, all the jacks have the same connection for positive and negative. This means that a battery pack would

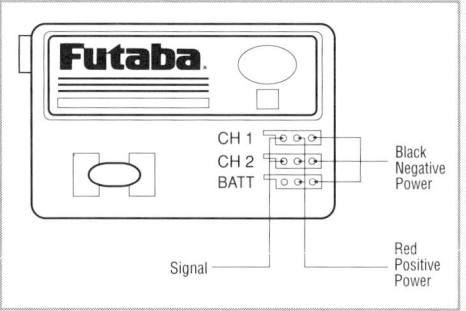

supply power to the receiver if it was plugged into the battery jack or into any other free jack. All the positive and negative pins are connected to the same trace on the circuit board. Knowing this, you can figure out which pins are which in the receiver. Plug a receiver battery wire into the receiver and note the location of the wires.

On a Futaba radio system, the pins on the far right of the receiver

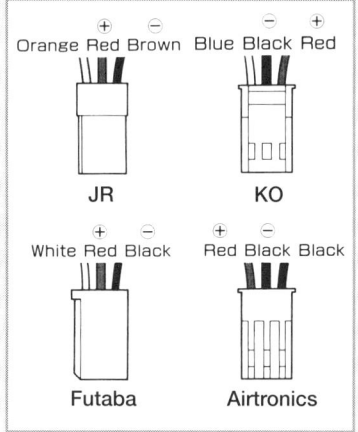

are the negative (black) power pins. Directly to the left of the negative pin is the positive (red) power pin. Again, all the pins above this pin are positive. Now that you know which are positive and negative, the only ones left are the signal pins.

If you try to use a JR servo on a Futaba receiver, the colors of the wires are different, but the order of the wire is the same. On a JR, the red wire is positive, the brown is negative, and the orange is signal. You might have to trim the plastic housing to fit into the receiver, but you don't have to rearrange the wire order. Just make sure the red wire is in the correct location and all the rest will be correct. Study the illustrations to figure out how the wires on different servos are arranged.

To change the configuration of the wires, you must first remove them from the connector. There are two ways the wires can be held in the plastic connectors, and how you remove them will depend on the type you have. On the end of each wire inside the plastic housing is a metal contact. This contact grips the pins in the receiver to make the electrical connection.

Sometimes, the metal contact has a small "barb-like" thing on it so that when it's inserted into the plastic housing it stays put. To remove this type, just find the metal barb, and press on it to bend it in. The wire will slide right out of the housing. Make sure you bend the barb back up so it will catch the housing again.

Sometimes, there's a similar kind of barb on the plastic housing that holds the contact in place. For this kind of connector, just lift the barb with the tip of a sharp knife and slide the wire out. The plastic will snap back into shape after you've removed the knife, so it doesn't need to be bent back.

After you've removed the wires, you can rearrange them so they match your particular receiver. Use a known servo or ESC plug, or the illustration (left) as a guide.

A channel 88, 75 MHz crystal.

that came with the radio. If you're on channel 80, you should stick within channels 75 and 85, and the closer the better.

It's important to know which band and type of radio you have before you buy new crystals. If you have a 27MHz radio, you must stick with 27MHz crystals, and the same is true of 75MHz. If you have an AM radio system, make sure the crystals are AM. FM/PCM crystals cost much more than AM crystals. Also, try to use crystals of the same make as your receiver and transmitter.

When you decide to buy a radio system, keep in mind what you need. If you just want a car to play around with, buy an inexpensive radio. If you know that you'll move up to a faster, more complicated car, you might want to buy a more expensive radio.

CHAPTER 5

Ni-Cd Batteries and Chargers

- How Ni-Cds work

- Types of cells

- Building battery packs

- Soldering basics

- Charging and discharging

CHAPTER 5

Ni-Cd batteries have revolutionized our world. You may not realize it, but they're everywhere—all over your house! If you have a cordless phone, a camcorder, a cordless drill, a Dustbuster, or a rechargeable flashlight, you have Ni-Cds. But even though they're common, few of us know how to take care of them.

How they Work

It's important to know that all Ni-Cd (nickel-cadmium) cells are rated at 1.2 volts. A pack might have "7.2 volts" on it, but it's really made up of six 1.2V cells connected in series. "In series" refers to the way in which the cells are wired together. If you've ever seen a flashlight that holds two D-cells in the barrel, you

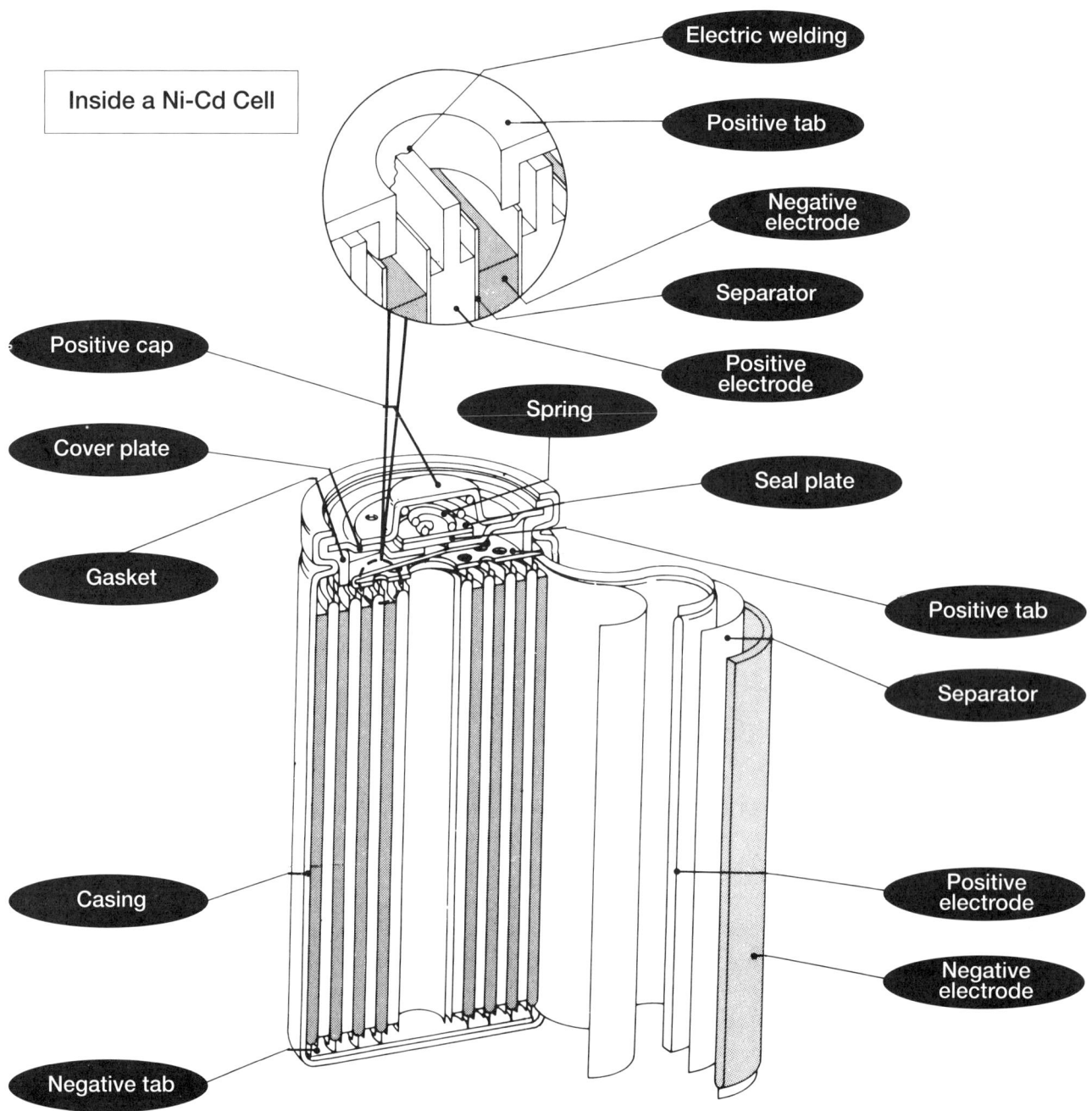

Inside a Ni-Cd Cell

NI-CD BATTERIES AND CHARGERS

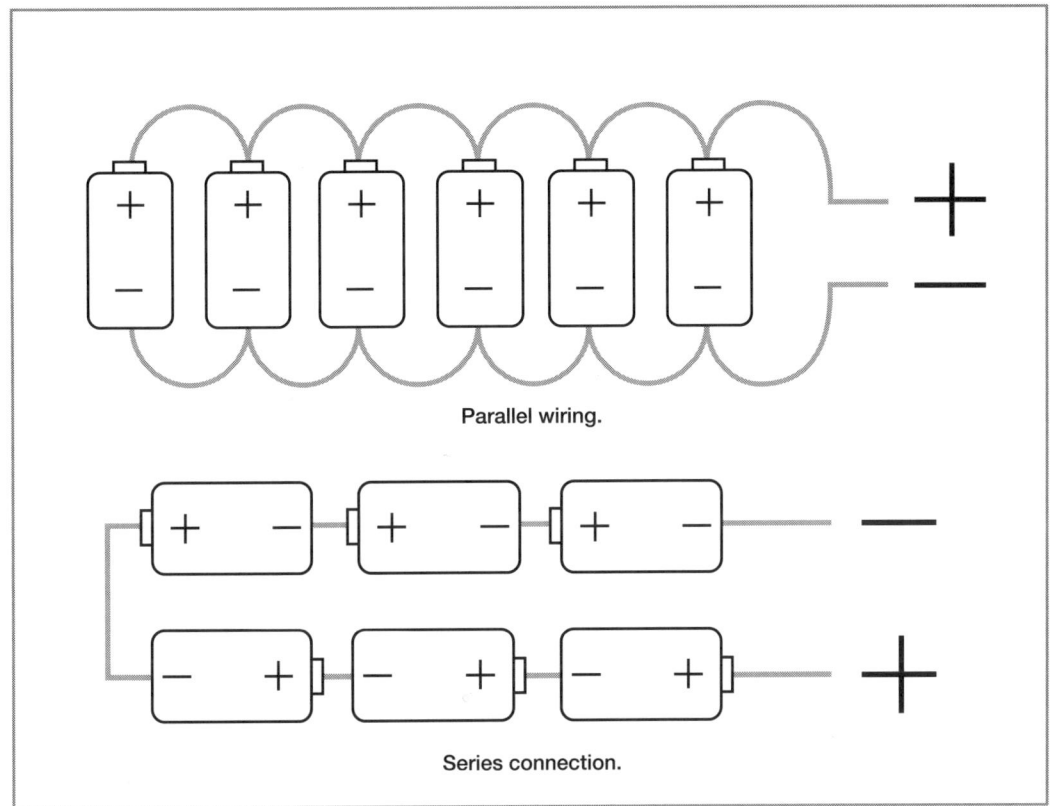

Battery pack configurations.

know what "series" is: the positive end of one cell is connected to the next cell's negative end. In a series connection, the voltage is totalled and the capacity (or amp/hour number) stays the same. Parallel wiring is when the cells' positive ends are joined and the negative ends are joined (see diagram). With a parallel connection, the voltage stays the same and the capacity (or amp/hour rating) is combined for each cell.

Ni-Cd cells are made up of layers of nickel and cadmium. A chemical reaction takes place when they're charged, and they store the electricity. When they're used, another chemical reaction converts the stored energy into voltage.

Many types of cells are used for R/C cars. Each meets a specific need and has its own charging requirements. The most popular size is the sub-C. It's slightly smaller than the C-size cell you might find in a flashlight. Sub-C cells are used for almost every type of R/C car, usually in a pack of six. The six cells are connected in series to gain a larger voltage.

SCR, SCE, SCRC?

Not only do Ni-Cd cells come in different sizes, but they also come with different capacities. Capacity is measured in milliamps per hour (mAh). A Sanyo 1200mAh SC battery is the same size as a 1700 SCRC, but their capacities are very different. The 1200 SC is old and outdated now, and I'm not even sure if it's made anymore. It was the industry standard for many years, but it has faded away.

• **SCRs.** The next wave in cells was SCR batteries. "R" stands for "rapid," as in rapid charge. The SCRs have thicker internal layers to allow fast charging. When they were first produced, they had a capacity of 1200mAh, but that was soon increased to 1400mAh. Another benefit was their slightly increased average volt-

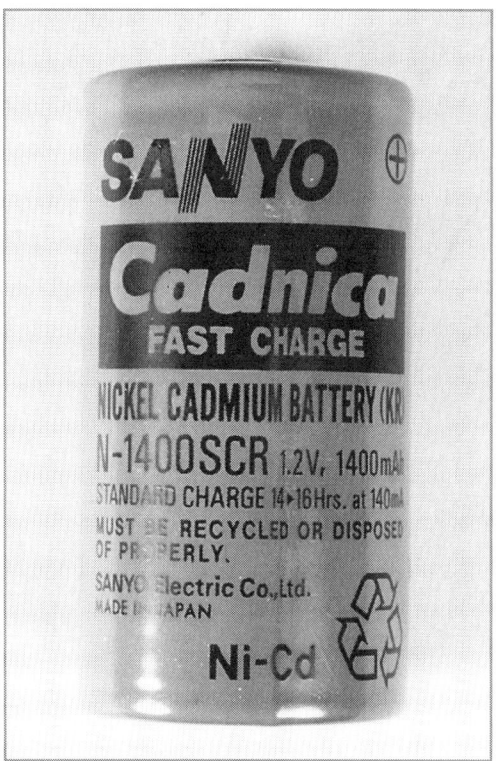

Sanyo's 1400 SCR.

Sanyo's 1700 SCRC.

age. Although it was only a few 10ths of a volt per cell, when six cells were joined, the increase was very noticeable. SCR cells are very tough and can be charged many times a day.

• **SCEs.** The next generation of batteries was the SCE 1700mAh. In an effort to increase capacity, designers gave the SCE more, but thinner, layers of nickel and cadmium. These batteries worked well, but they were more fragile and had to be charged, discharged and stored carefully, or they wouldn't last long or perform well. The SCE had a slightly lower average voltage than the SCR, but this could be overcome by gearing up to take advantage of the added capacity.

SCE cells turned out to be much more fragile than the tough SCR cells. SCRs can be charged at 5 to 9 amps without damaging the cells. SCE cells had to be charged at 3½ amps, and many people believed that a pack should be run only once a week. SCR cells could be run repeatedly without seeming to suffer, but their run times were still less than those of the SCEs.

Well, just as I had figured, Sanyo took the next logical step and developed the SCRC—fast charge and 1700mAh! These cells have all the capacity of the SCEs with the voltage and strength of the SCRs. Today, these are the ultimate cells for R/C cars.

Packs and Loose Cells

When you go to the hobby shop to look for a battery pack for your car, you have a few choices to make. Most cars will require a stick-type pack that's made up of two rows of three cells. These packs come assembled, covered with heat-shrink plastic and with what has become the standard connector for the majority of car kits: the Tamiya connector. You can find all the different types of cells—from 1200mAh to 1700mAh—in stick packs.

Some on-road and off-road cars aren't designed to use stick packs. For those

NI-CD BATTERIES AND CHARGERS

Soldering Basics

Soldering is an art. To get a good solder joint, you must have a good iron, the right solder and, as with everything else, practice. What's a good iron? It depends on what you plan to do with it. For delicate, printed-circuit-board soldering, any small pencil-type iron will do; but if you want to build battery packs and solder wires to motors, you'll need an iron that has at least 50 watts of power. Generally, the hotter, the better.

When you solder cells together to make a battery pack, you must heat up each cell enough to make the solder flow onto it. The problem is that the cell acts like a giant heat sink and actually cools the iron. Leaving the iron in one place while you wait for it to heat up isn't good for the cells, so you have to use a strong iron and solder quickly.

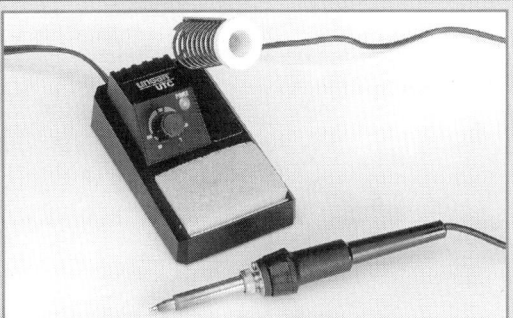
Ungar's Super Race Station.

Building a Battery Pack

Often, a set of matched cells comes loose in a bag; the manufacturer leaves the assembly up to you. To assemble a pack, you'll need some battery bars or braid, solder, glue, silicone-insulated wires and a set of connectors. A battery-building jig can also be helpful; with one, you can solder the cells before you glue them.

If you aren't using a jig, start by gluing the cells together. (I use Shoe-Goo because it's strong, yet I can remove it later if I have to.) Lay the cells on their sides on a flat surface. Alternate the direction of the cells so no two adjoining cells are going in the same direction. Run a small line of glue along the edge of each cell where it contacts another cell, and assemble the group of cells on the flat surface. Keep all the cells

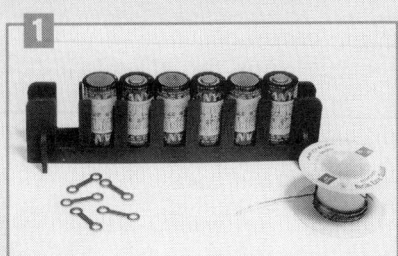

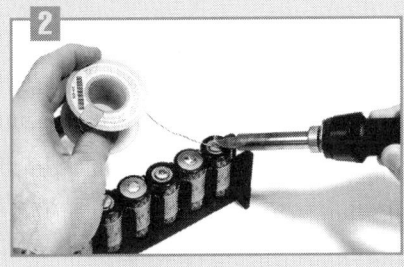

together with two books or blocks of wood on either end, and make sure that they're all aligned. It's best to let this type of glue dry overnight.

Now you can start to solder the connections between the cells. Heat the iron, and clean the ends of each of the cells. (A simple twist with a piece of sandpaper on each end is enough.)

1. Set the pack on end so that one set of the positive and negative ends of the cells is facing upward, or use the jig. Apply some solder to the iron's tip, and make sure that it melts easily.

2. Hold the broad side of the tip onto one of the cells' ends, and apply some solder. It should flow easily and harden with a shiny finish. Apply a small amount of solder to each cell's end (this is known as "pre-tinning"), flip the pack over, and repeat.

With the cells pre-tinned, it's much easier to solder the battery bars between the cells.

3. Starting at one end of the pack, place a bar between the first and second cells. Hold the bar firmly in place with a hobby knife, and apply the iron to the solder on one of the batteries. The solder should melt on the cell and run between it and the bar. You might want

to add a little more solder to ensure a solid joint. Repeat the process with the other end of the same bar. Join the next two cells with another bar, and repeat the process with the next two. You'll then have three sets of cells joined with bars.

4. Flip the pack over and place a bar between the second and third cells; add another bar between the fourth and fifth cells, and you'll have a complete circuit.

5. The two outside cells will each have one end that's not connected to a bar; these are the positive and negative connection for the pack. Attach the wires of your connector to these points, but make sure they're long enough to reach the connectors on your car. If you used a jig and didn't glue the cells first, you can do it now.

GETTING STARTED IN R/C CARS 45

CHAPTER 5

Left: pack built using battery bars. Right: a standard 6-cell stick pack.

vehicles, you must build a pack with loose cells, which are sold in packs of four, six and seven, and they're usually matched.

Matched Cells

When you assemble a group of batteries into a pack, they're each responsible for a portion of the pack's total power. Like the saying about a chain being only as strong as its weakest link, a pack is only as strong as its weakest cell. To ensure that they all perform equally well, many companies run thousands of cells through a series of charges and discharges to rate them (this is called "cycling"). Most companies use a standard series of settings against which packs are compared. The cells are charged and then discharged to a voltage of 0.9 volt per cell, which has become the industry standard cutoff voltage for a single cell. The rate of discharge varies, but 20 amps seems to be the most common. After being tested, each cell is labeled with a sticker that denotes its performance rating.

The most important rating is run time in seconds. With each pack being discharged at 20 amps to a voltage of 0.9 volt, looking at the packs' time rating will tell you which has a greater capacity. The greater the capacity, the longer the run time. Remember: although the time is important, the discharge amp rate will have a great deal to do with the numbers. A pack that was discharged at 10 amps for 600 seconds is equal to a pack that was discharged at 20 amps for 300 seconds.

Average voltage is next in importance. A cell's average voltage is about 1.1 to 1.14 volts. By their nature, SCR and SCRC cells have a slightly higher voltage than SCE cells.

After the cells have been rated, they can be grouped with similar cells to form a matched pack. A matched pack will dump (die) very suddenly, because all the cells will dump at the same time. This is good and bad. On the good side, the pack puts out full power before dumping, and it doesn't go into a slow-motion mode for the last 30 to 60 seconds. The bad part is

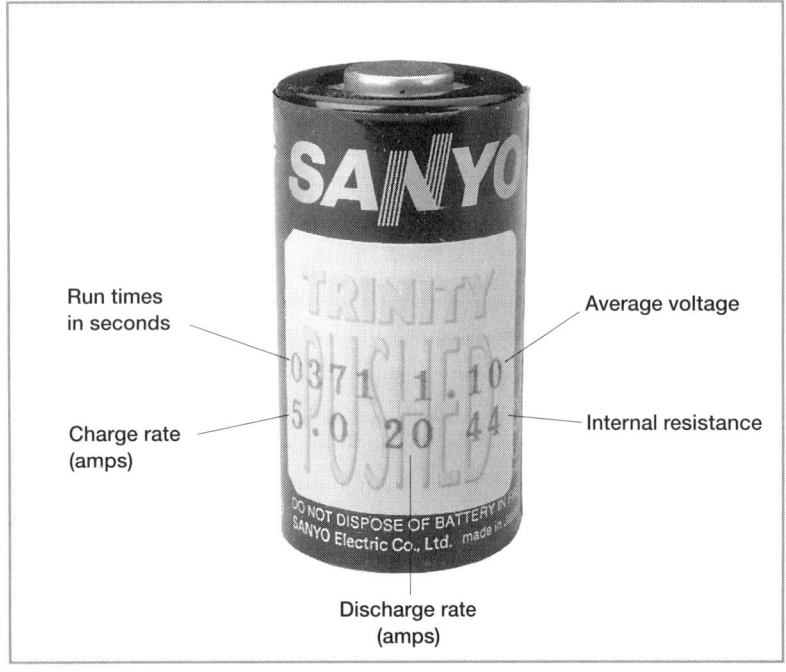

Battery-matching label.

NI-CD BATTERIES AND CHARGERS

that they dump with little warning. I've been at races in which a car that was turning 10-second laps on one lap was completely dead on the next lap. Gearing becomes crucial to winning a 4-minute race.

Discharging

Ni-Cd batteries are great when treated properly, but they can be very temperamental if abused. Like the proverbial elephant, a Ni-Cd battery has a memory. If you don't use the complete charge before you recharge, the pack will begin to "remember" how much it was discharged. If this partial discharging is repeated continually, the pack will eventually no longer be able to complete a full discharge cycle. It will only discharge to a certain point, so it will have a short run time. Cordless phones are known for this, because most people don't use the whole battery cycle; the phone rests on a charger perpetually. After a year or two, the pack is just shot because it was never fully cycled.

When racing, most of us use every last drop of power from the pack, and that's good. Some companies make a battery tray that will discharge each cell in a pack to a certain voltage after a race. As a beginner, just make sure you use as much of the charge as you can before you recharge the pack.

Chargers

Today, several types of chargers are available, ranging in price from $10 to $300. The least expensive type is an overnight charger, but few people use them now.

• **Fast chargers.** These will fully charge a pack in about 15 minutes. The simplest fast chargers have a dial timer that you set for 15 minutes. It simply delivers power to the pack until the timer shuts it off. These chargers work, but they can be unsafe if they're used incorrectly. The charger has no way of "knowing" whether you've hooked up a pack that has already been charged, and it will continue to charge until it or the pack burns up. To get the most out of a charger with a timer, keep a close watch on the battery's temperature. As it reaches full charge, the temperature will rise. If the timer shuts the charger off, but the pack isn't warm, give it another 5 minutes, but keep your hand on the pack. When the pack is warm, it's ready to go. Some chargers may take as long as 25 minutes to fully charge a pack.

• **Peak-detection chargers.** These shut off automatically when the pack is fully charged. As a Ni-Cd pack is charged, its voltage rises. The voltage continues to rise until the pack is fully charged, and then it begins to fall slowly. The peak of

A discharging tray will discharge the cells to equal voltage.

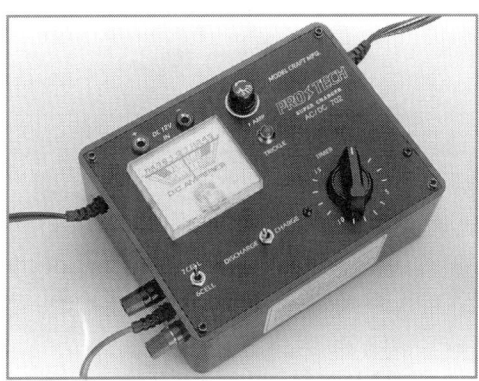

A simple timer-controlled fast charger.

CHAPTER 5

Battery Connectors

There are many types of connectors, each with their own features—and manufacturers' claims about their efficiency. Though several are very good at transferring power, I think one is the best: the Litespeed*—or Sermos—connector. I use this connector mainly because it's efficent, but I also like it because it's easy to use and it's cost-effective.

Most connectors are sold in pairs: one "male" and one "female". Each half of the connector accommodates both the positive and the negative wires. To set up one car, you need a male half for the speed control and a female half for the pack. But when you buy your fourth or fifth battery and end up with a handful of extra male connectors, you realize that there's a problem!

Sermos connectors were designed differently; each connector fits an identical connector (no male or female). They're also designed as a single conductor unit with separate connectors for positive and negative. Red and black housings help you tell positive from negative and are also splined so that two can be joined to form a positive/negative connector.

1. It's important to connect Sermos connectors correctly. Start

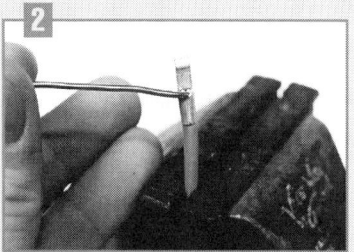

by stripping away about ⅓ inch of the wire's insulation. Twist the strands together and insert them into the metal connector tip. Clamp the wire lightly in a vise with the connector sticking straight up.

2. To get started, apply solder to the side of the tube portion of the connector with a hot iron, and then start to flow solder into the top and bottom of the tube. Be careful not to get any solder on the end of the connector that makes contact with another connector. The wires inside will begin to suck up the solder as they get hot. When the connector stops accepting solder, let it sit for a couple of minutes to cool. If you try to move it too soon, you'll ruin the solder joint.

3. Insert the cooled wire into the plastic housing of the correct color until you hear a snap. You're ready to go!

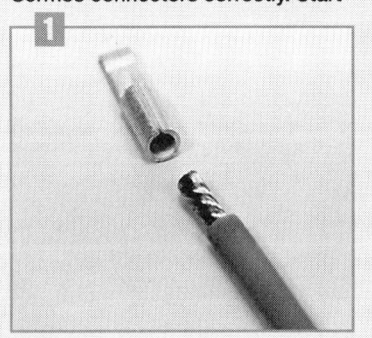

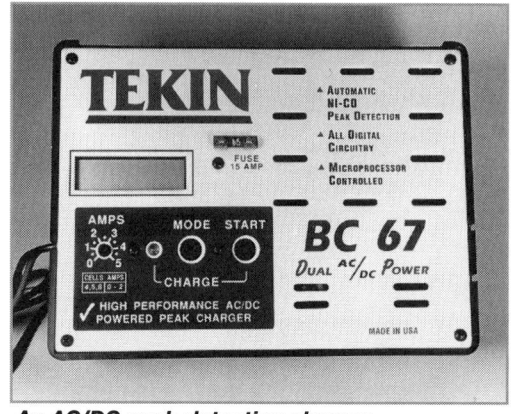

An AC/DC peak-detection charger.

Chargers are either AC- or DC-powered, so they have to be hooked up to a power source. Some can simply be plugged into a wall outlet; some can be plugged into a car's cigarette lighter; and some work with both. DC-only chargers are usually smaller and lighter than AC chargers.

Most peak chargers are DC, because voltage fluctuations in AC can cause false peaking, which will prematurely stop the charging. It's hard to say that one source is better, because it all depends on your needs. I guess the best bet is to get an AC/DC charger!

Twelve volts of DC current can also be supplied indoors by a power supply. Power supplies regulate the AC power and stabilize it for a steady 12V DC supply. Power supplies are used mostly by racers who go to tracks that have AC power in the pits.

So there you have it. Now you know a little about Ni-Cds and how to take care of them. When you buy a new pack, decide what you want from it. If you race, you might want to invest in a really good pack, but for fun running, you'd be better off with several sport packs.

that rise and fall is what tells the charger to stop the charging. You can do the same thing yourself with a timer charger and a digital voltmeter. Simply connect the red DVM wire to the pack's positive, and the black wire to the pack's negative; then just watch the voltage readings for the peak voltage.

CHAPTER 6

Gas Cars, Trucks and Engines

- Off-road and on-road
- How engines work
- Engine maintenance
- Engine break-in and tuning
- Fuel and accessories

CHAPTER 6

Although we say "gas-powered," most R/C cars are never run on gasoline. The fuel used in most R/C cars is a blend of alcohol, nitromethane and oil. There are just as many (and maybe more!) types of gas-powered vehicles as there are electric ones. They offer the same performance features that electric vehicles do, but they usually run faster and longer. Gas-powered vehicles are, however, more difficult to operate. To become familiar with basic suspension and radio operation, beginners should start with electric vehicles. A model engine adds an entirely new dimension to your enjoyment of R/C cars. If you have experience with electric models and you want a new challenge, go nitro!

OFF-ROAD

- **1/8-scale buggies.** The most popular category of off-road gas vehicles is probably 1/8-scale 4WD buggy. You'll know why they're so popular once you've seen one run at 40-plus miles per hour! They're powered by .21ci engines that are capable of putting out 2hp. The drive system usually consists of three differentials that deliver power to each of the wheels through drive shafts. Braking is achieved with the throttle servo and a disk-brake system. Some cars use a single disk; others use twin disks for more stopping power.

Almost every nitro-powered car comes with a flip-top fuel tank that can be filled in seconds. Electric car races usually last 4 minutes—the duration of one battery pack—but gas races can last as long as an hour, and you need a fast, simple method of refueling.

- **1/8-scale trucks.** Eighth-scale nitro trucks are a new breed of R/C cars. They're basically just buggies that have been outfitted with truck tires and truck bodies, but even these simple modifications change handling drastically. The larger tires raise the truck's center of gravity and, because they have a higher profile, the tires flex more in the turns. You have to use a different style of driving from the one you would use with a buggy. The larger tires are great for rough surfaces though, because of the increased ground clearance.

- **1/10-scale trucks.** A few years ago, Kyosho introduced the Rampage—a 1/10-scale, 2WD truck that got the country started on gas truck racing. It was basically an electric truck chassis that had a .12 engine instead of an electric motor. Soon afterward, conversions for the Associated and Losi electric trucks began to show up,

GAS CARS, TRUCKS AND ENGINES

1/10 scale truck — OFF-ROAD

and, because of their sophisticated suspensions, lap times went down. Since then, the category has grown into one of the biggest in the country. Right now, trucks are made by Associated, Traxxas, Kyosho, Schumacher and Flying Point*, and there are also several conversions. Because they're based on their electric cousins, $1/10$-scale trucks are a great way to get into gas racing.

• **$1/10$-scale 4WD buggies.** A new breed of 4WD buggy has arrived: cars such as the Kyosho Inferno 10, the Pirate* 10 and the Schumacher Nitro 10 are smaller versions of the big $1/8$-scale buggies. They have the same components as the bigger cars (but they're slightly smaller), and they're powered by smaller, .12 engines. They're a little more complicated than 2WD vehicles, but they're a good step up from your first gas car.

• **$1/10$-scale 2WD buggies.** A few gas-powered 2WD buggies are available: Traxxas makes a $1/10$-scale, 2WD buggy that's based on its popular Nitro Hawk truck and has smaller wheels and a buggy body; Kyosho offers a buggy called the Rampage Pro; and Flying Point has a buggy called the Pizzazz. This is yet another new class of racing that might become as popular as the trucks.

ON-ROAD

• **$1/8$-scale cars.** Eighth-scale, on-road gas cars are the "Formula 1" of R/C. Like the off-road buggies, these cars are powered by .21 engines and are either 2WD or 4WD. Some of these cars have 2- or 3-speed transmissions that allow them to reach speeds of 70mph!

These cars' drive systems are usually a combination of gears, shafts and belts.

1/10 4WD buggy — OFF-ROAD

1/10 2WD buggy — OFF-ROAD

CHAPTER 6

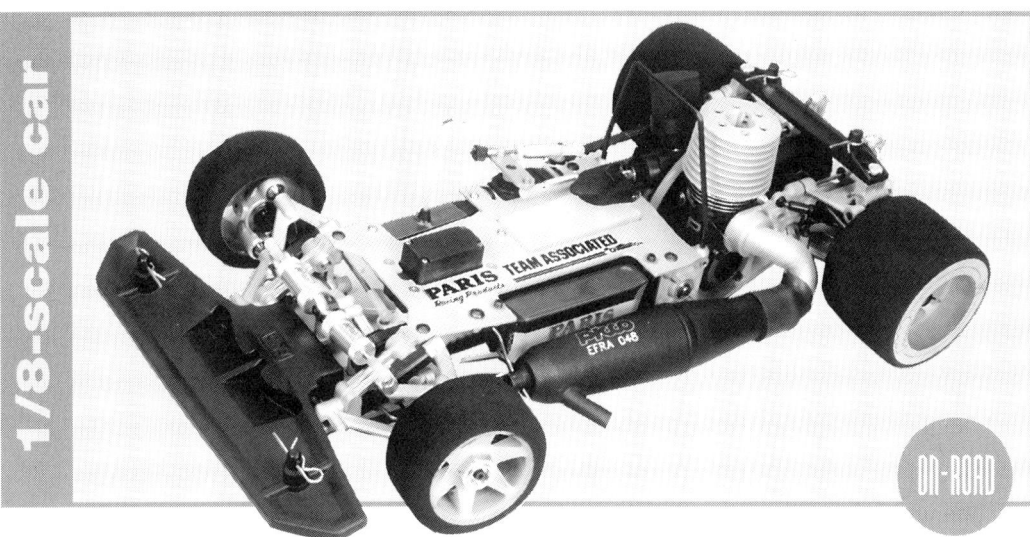

1/8-scale car — ON-ROAD

Chassis range from simple flat-pan chassis to complex 4W, independent-suspension machines. All 1/8-scale cars are for experienced drivers. Believe me, you'll have more fun with them when you know what you're doing.

• **1/10-scale cars.** Over the past couple of years, gas on-road racing has shifted toward 1/10 scale. Several makers of 1/8-scale cars shrank their designs into 1/10 scale. These cars are just like the 1/8-scale cars, but they use .15 engines and they cost less.

Another form of 1/10-scale on-road racing has also emerged. Dynamite's* Apex 10 is based on Bolink electric pan-car parts. It uses most of the parts available for electric cars, yet it can run as fast as 40mph! Conversions are also available for those of you who already have an Associated 10L car lying around. This is perhaps the cheapest way to get into gas on-road racing.

• **Go-karts.** In 1994, Kyosho introduced a great new vehicle—the nitro-powered go-kart. It's powered by a pull-start .10 engine, and it's as easy as can be to build and operate. Like the full-size go-karts, it has no suspension and no diff. Power is delivered to the rear wheels through gears and a chain, and a rear disk brake stops the kart with authority. They're great for beginners and advanced modelers.

1/10-scale car — ON-ROAD

Go-kart — ON-ROAD

52 GETTING STARTED IN R/C CARS

How Engines Work

Small model engines are amazing. They have so few parts, yet they run very well and put out gobs of power. Most of the engines used in R/C cars are 2-stroke. Two-stroke engines have an intake/compression stroke and a ignition/exhaust stroke, but no valves.

To start an engine, you first have to attach a battery to the glow plug. (The glow plug is like a spark plug but, as its name implies, it glows.) Then you turn the engine over using a pull-starter or an electric starter motor. As the engine turns over, fuel is drawn from the tank and sucked into the carburetor, where it mixes with air. The fuel/air mixture then enters a small

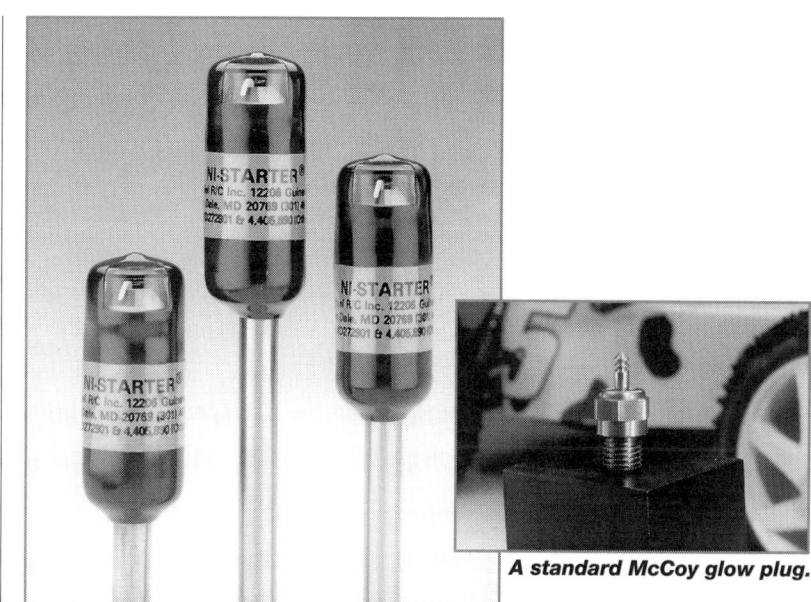

Various Ni-starters made by McDaniel*.

A standard McCoy glow plug.

Typical 2-stroke model car engine (exploded view).

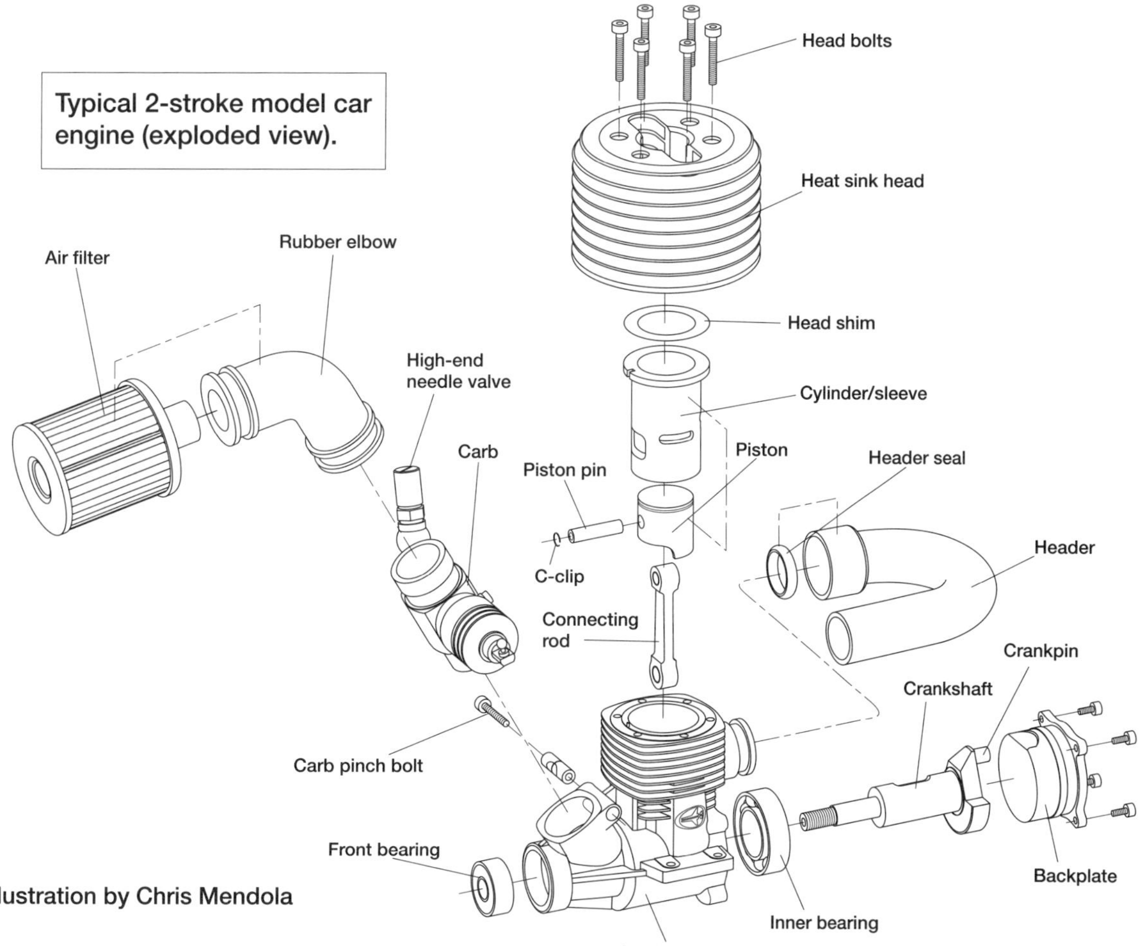

Illustration by Chris Mendola

CHAPTER 6

"window" in the crankshaft, travels to the inside of the engine, and ends up in the combustion chamber, where it's compressed by the rising piston. When the piston reaches the top of the cylinder, the mixture explodes and forces the piston back down. As the piston travels downward, the exhaust is blown out of the engine through a port in the side of the cylinder. When the piston reaches its lowest point, it begins to rise again as the crankshaft rotates. The small window in the crankshaft opens again, bringing in a new load of fuel to burn. Once this cycle has started, you can remove the glow-plug battery without causing the engine to die.

Engine Care and Maintenance

The better you take care of your engine, the longer it will last. Fuel left inside the engine will attract moisture and will damage the bearings. To prevent this from happening, perform a little maintenance after each run. First, run the tank dry. When the engine quits, try to start it again without adding more fuel. It may sputter for a few seconds, but that should be it. Remove the air filter, and shoot some after-run oil into the carb. To distribute the oil evenly, crank the engine over a couple of times with the starter. I usually add a few more drops of oil and turn it over by hand. And that's it! If you follow these simple steps after each run, your engine will stay in tiptop shape.

Rebuilding Your Engine

After several hours of use, your engine might look like a big chunk of baked dirt and oil. It's a good idea to remove as much of this as you can with a stiff brush between runs, but sooner or later, you'll want to completely rebuild it to make it look like new again. First, remove the engine from the car and remove the pipe. Keep the header in place, but plug the opening with a piece of paper towel. With the air filter on, remove as much of the dirt as you can with a brush. Remove the clutch and flywheel assembly and set it aside, then loosen the head bolts. Be careful with your selection of hex wrenches! Most Japanese and European engines use metric hardware; some use standard U.S. hardware. Make sure that the wrench fits tightly so you don't strip the bolt head. Remove the head and the backplate, and set the two aside. The backplate might have a thin paper gasket; be careful with it and be sure you don't rip it; you'll need to use it again.

Insert your finger into the cylinder and push the piston down. Grab one of the ports with your finger and try to pull the sleeve straight out. If it's tight, twist it slightly, but don't use any tools! If you can't get it to budge, insert the tip of a plastic tie-wrap or popsicle stick into the sleeve, and stick it slightly into the

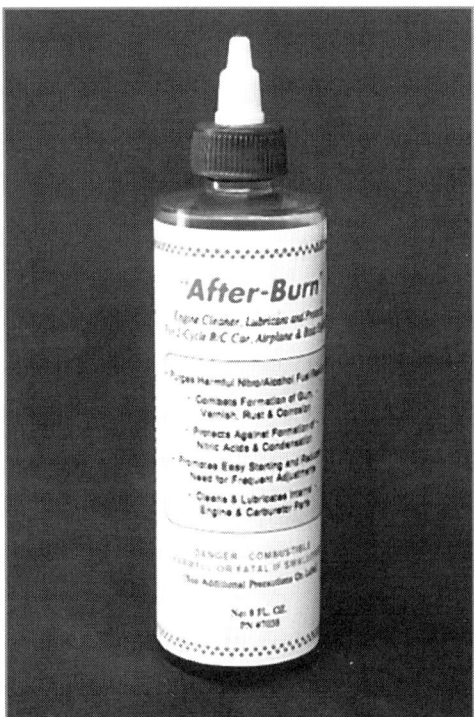

After-run oil keeps your engine in tip-top shape between runs.

Starters and Starter Boxes

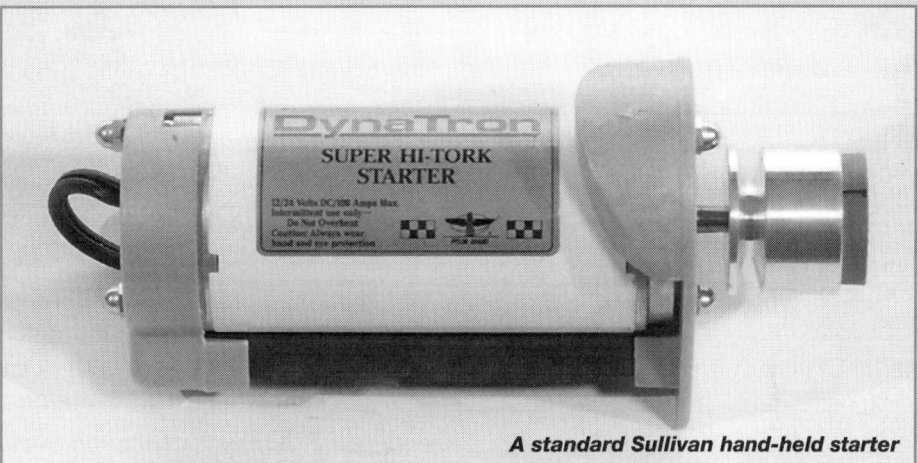

A standard Sullivan hand-held starter

An electric starter is nothing more than an electric motor. When you bump the starter's rubber wheel against an engine's flywheel, it turns the engine over. All engines run counterclockwise, so the rubber wheel has to spin clockwise. Make sure the wheel turns the flywheel in the right direction! Also take into consideration the direction from which direction you start the car, and the polarity of the starter.

I always start my engines with the clutch and flywheel toward me. That means that my starter wheel must turn clockwise when applied from the front of the engine. A note about rubber starter wheels: glue the rubber to the hub with superglue, and make sure you tighten the hub on the shaft. Believe me, it's no fun to run after a rubber starter wheel when it spins itself off the starter (they move!).

Another version of the electric starter is the starter box. As its name implies, it's a starter motor in a box. Part of the starter wheel sticks through an opening in the top of the box. You set the car on top of the box, where it's held in alignment with the starter by a couple of posts. When you press down on the car, it hits the starter switch, and the engine flips over. Starter boxes make starting a one-hand operation!

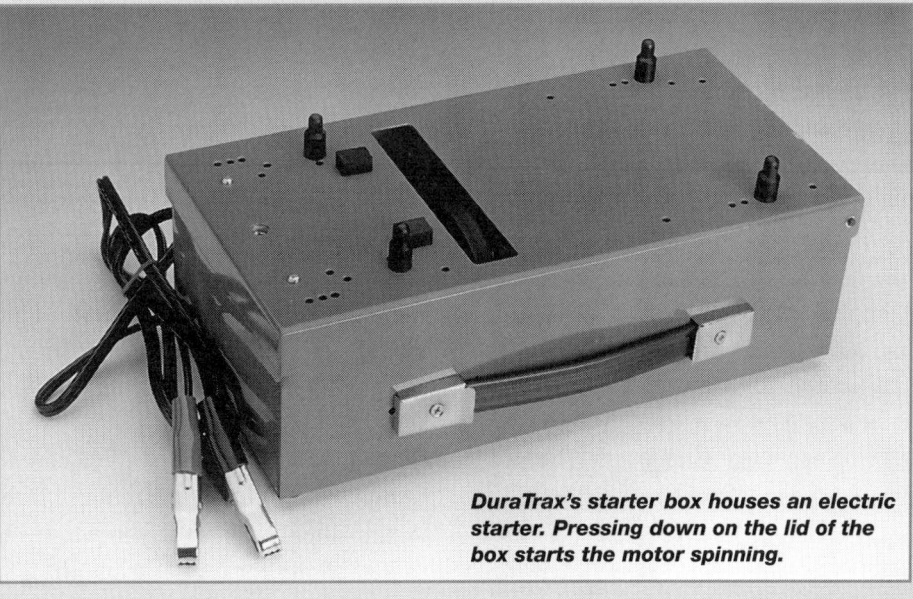

DuraTrax's starter box houses an electric starter. Pressing down on the lid of the box starts the motor spinning.

exhaust port. Turn the engine over slowly. The piston will rise, grab the tie-wrap, and force the sleeve up. This will raise it only slightly; the rest is up to your finger.

With the sleeve out, the piston will have enough room inside the engine to move around a lot. Carefully turn the engine over so that the backplate side is facing straight down. Give it a little shake, and the piston and connecting rod should fall off the crankshaft and slide out of the engine. With the piston removed, the crankshaft will slide right out. Finish the teardown by removing the carb and header. Clean the crankshaft, sleeve and piston/connecting rod with electric-motor cleaning spray, and re-lube them right away. It's a good idea to put them in separate ziplock bags for safekeeping.

It isn't always necessary to remove the bearings from the case, but it makes cleaning easier. Two engine bearings (front and inner) are press-fit into the aluminum case, and to get them out, you must use heat.

Kids, get help from your parents for the next few steps! Put the crankcase in an oven (a toaster oven works well) set at 350 degrees for about 10 minutes. Remove the crankcase with a pot holder, and lightly bang the backplate side on another pot holder that's lying on a hard surface, such as a cutting board or countertop. Hold the case firmly, and let the heel of your hand, not the engine, hit the surface. This should be enough force to pop it right out. Turn the engine over and repeat the process for the front bearing. If the bearings don't come out, heat the engine a little longer.

When the bearings are out of the case, clean them with motor spray. I scrub the case with a toothbrush dipped in soapy water. Clean the head and backplate with soapy water, and try to remove as much of the dirt between the fins as you can. Spray the carb with motor spray, add a drop or two of oil to the barrel, and you've finished.

To reassemble the engine, reverse the order of the teardown. To install the bearings easily, heat the case again. Slide the inner bearing onto the crankshaft, and slide the whole thing into the hot case. The bearing should drop right into its space. Slide the crankshaft out again, and put the front bearing over the end of it, seal first. Use the crankshaft to insert the front bearing. If the bearings are aligned properly, the crankshaft will slide into the case with no effort. Oil the bearings and the piston and sleeve. Make sure that you've installed the piston in the same way as it was installed before you removed it. The connecting rod usually has a tiny hole drilled into the bottom end for lubrication. Make sure that this hole is facing the crankshaft.

It's easiest to get the sleeve in when the piston is at top dead center. Carefully insert the sleeve into the case until it touches the piston. Align the piston and the sleeve with your fingers, and slowly press the sleeve in, using a slight twisting motion. It should slide in smoothly, so stop if you feel any resistance. On some engines, such as the O.S.* CZ-R and CZ-Z, the wristpin that holds the piston on the connecting rod can slide back and forth; if it does, you won't be able to insert the sleeve. Make sure it's centered and stays put while you assemble the engine.

When you insert the bolts, thread them in only until you feel a slight bit of resistance. When they're all in, tighten one and then tighten the one opposite it. Make sure that all the bolts are firmly tightened.

Air Filters

One of the simplest things you can do to protect your engine is to use a filter. An air filter is a must if you want your engine to run for longer than just a tank of fuel. Without a filter, dirt, dust and bugs will eventually find their way into the

GAS CARS, TRUCKS AND ENGINES

Left: a foam air filter. Right: a foam pre-filter.

engine and cause the parts to wear out prematurely. There are a few types of air filters, and each has different maintenance requirements.

• **Paper.** A paper filter is made of porous paper that's folded like an accordion to get lots of material into a small shape. Paper filters shouldn't get wet or soaked with fuel or oil, and they aren't great for use in very dusty areas.

• **Foam.** If used properly, foam filters are very good at trapping dirt and dust. To be truly effective, a foam filter must be oiled to help it trap dirt. The stickier the oil, the better! The best stuff I've found is K&N Foam Filter Oil. It's made for full-size foam filters, and it can be ordered from any good auto-parts store. One huge bottle costs less than $10.

• **Pre-wraps.** To help paper filters cope better with the fine stuff, many people use a foam pre-filter. A foam sleeve fits over the paper element and can be oiled to trap dirt. The good thing about pre-filters is that you can store them all oiled up, so you can easily replace one after a few runs.

Fuel Filters

Dirt and grime can also get into your engine through the fuel lines. Dust and dirt can find its way into your fuel bottle and

Foam air filter.

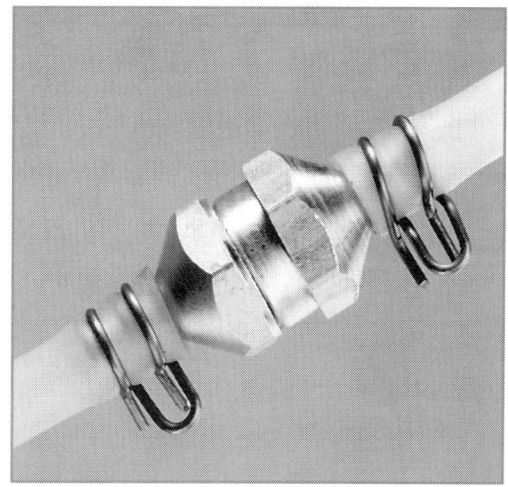

Du-Bro* fuel filter.

CHAPTER 6

Associated's RC10GT uses a paper element covered by a foam filter.

into your fuel tank, where it eventually gets sucked into your engine. To prevent this from happening, install a fuel filter between the tank and the engine. This small device has a fuel-line fitting on each end. Fuel entering the filter must pass through a fine-mesh screen before it exits to the carb. Dirt particles will be trapped in the filter and will never reach the engine.

After you've run about a gallon of fuel, clean the filter by forcing fuel through in the opposite direction. I forgot to clean a filter once, and it started to limit the amount of fuel that could reach the engine, causing it to run lean.

Starting and Breaking In

Starting and tuning a gas engine is very tricky. Some engines will jump to life on the first try, and others need patience to get going. The first things you need are a fresh bottle of fuel, a fully charged glow-plug driver and a starter motor with a rubber wheel. If your engine comes with a pull-start, you'll use that.

After you've filled the tank, press the primer button (if your tank has one) or turn the engine over a couple of times with the starter cord or the electric starter so that fuel travels up the fuel line. Connect the glow-plug battery and turn the engine over. If you have a pull-start engine, give its cord a few quick, short yanks to get it fired. Don't over-extend the cord, or it might come right out of the engine. If you have an electric starter, turn it on and get it up to speed. Make sure the starter wheel is spinning in the right direction. Bump the starter wheel against the flywheel and hold it in place. A brand-new engine might have so much compression that it's almost impossible to turn it over. If this is the case, loosen the glow plug slightly to reduce the engine's compression. Using an electric starter takes a while to master, so don't get discouraged!

When the engine starts up, remove the starter quickly. If the car is on its side, turn it upright. Give the throttle a couple of blips to get the engine cleared out. If all seems well, send it out for a break-in run. It usually takes at least four tanks of fuel to break in an engine. To check the main needle setting, count how many turns from being closed it is. A good starting range is between two and three turns out. The car should run very slowly and sound "blubbery." You should see smoke and oil coming from the exhaust pipe. As long as the top speed is very mild and you see a lot of smoke, you can be sure that the engine is running very rich, which is good for the break-in period.

As you go through your first few tanks, you'll begin to notice an increase in performance as the parts break in properly. Try to vary the engine's revs, but don't let it rev for too long. By the time I've gone though a full five tanks, I'm ready to tune to scream.

Tuning

There are several ways to tell whether your engine has been properly tuned. The most important is its temperature. When an engine is set too lean (more air, less

GAS CARS, TRUCKS AND ENGINES

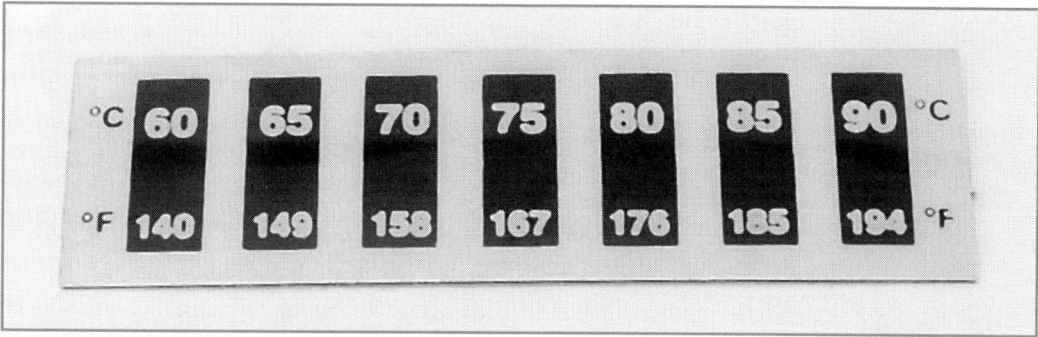

CRC's Temp Tape.

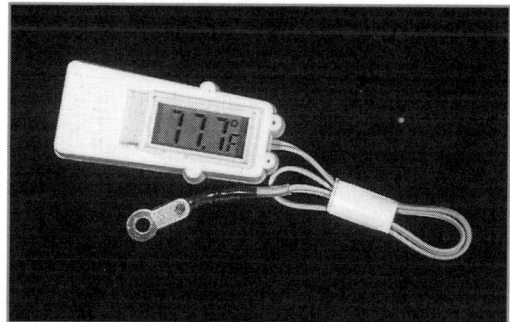

MIP's on-board temp gauge.

fuel), you get tremendous power, but there isn't enough fuel and oil to carry away the engine's heat. If the engine continues to be run in this state, its temperature can rise to more than 300 degrees—not good! An engine's temperature will range from 100 to 300-plus degrees. A good range to shoot for is between 200 and 240 degrees, but remember that engine temperature can be affected by the weather, the air flow and the type of engine, fuel, or plug you have, so there isn't one "right" temp. With practice, you'll learn to find a good setting; just learn how to spot a hot situation. The simplest way to gauge the temp of an engine is the "spit test." Spit on the engine's head. If it boils and crackles violently, the engine is on the hot side; if it slowly bubbles and remains on the head for a while, it's OK. Another good way to judge temp is with CRC's* Temp Tape. It displays a range of temperatures in 10-degree increments. MIP's* temp gauge has a small probe that's bolted onto the engine's head and relays the temp to the unit's LCD display. The best solution is very expensive, but effective: a temp gun, such as the one by Raytek*, measures temperature without even touching the engine.

But besides all the temp stuff, you can tell how the engine is tuned by listening and watching. First, be sure you see bluish smoke. I always start with the full-speed needle set rich and work my way lean a

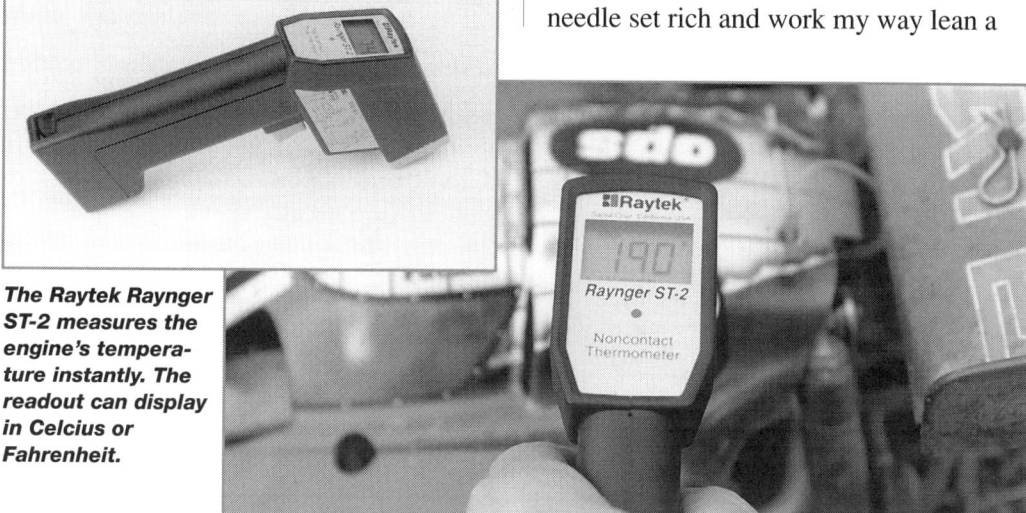

The Raytek Raynger ST-2 measures the engine's temperature instantly. The readout can display in Celcius or Fahrenheit.

GETTING STARTED IN R/C CARS 59

CHAPTER 6

little at a time. You'll know when it's tuned correctly. If the engine gets too hot, it will sound very hollow.

The low-end needle controls the air/fuel mixture at idle and at low speeds. Its setting determines how an engine idles and how the transition to a higher speed is made. The low-end needle is usually set at the factory, and only a slight adjustment will be needed to get it right. To test the low-end setting, start your engine and bring it up to temp by letting it run for a minute or so. Rev the engine a couple of times to clean it out, and let it settle for about 10 seconds. Pinch off the fuel line as close to the carb nipple as possible. If your low end is too lean (more air than fuel) the engine will shut off almost instantly. If it's rich (more fuel than air) it will do nothing for about 5 seconds, then it will rev up, and then it will really rev and die. Try to keep the setting on the rich side, and tune the engine so that you get a good response when you punch the throttle from a dead stop.

Pipes

Just like full-size engines, model engines need mufflers, or pipes. Because we use 2-stroke engines, we can tune the exhaust system to suit our needs. Some pipes are designed for the larger .21 engines, and others are for the smaller .12 and .15 engines.

If your car comes with a pipe, use it. Most offer great performance and don't need to be replaced. Some cars use a simple airplane-type muffler that isn't tuned and can be replaced for better performance. Choose a pipe that's designed to suit the size of your engine. Tuning a pipe is a matter of adjusting the length of the exhaust system. The length is measured from the center of the cylinder diameter to the widest part of the pipe. Generally speaking, with a longer pipe, you'll get more punch; use a shorter one for higher top-end power.

Fuel

When you choose fuel, try to buy one that was designed specifically for cars. Blue

Various .21 pipes.

Blue Thunder car fuel.

Engine Troubleshooting

If your engine...

Runs erratically, or hot

Fuel foaming
Bad plug gasket
Fuel line too small
Leaking glow-plug stem
Glow plug shortened
Blocked fuel vent
Glow plug blown
Pick-up off in tank
Bad fuel
Crack in crankcase
Air leak in tank
Varnish in engine
Air leak in line
Bearings worn out
Kinked fuel line
Bearings defective
Debris in fuel line
Split tubing inside tank
Carb leaking air
Carb set too lean
Debris in filter
Loose case screws
Clogged needle valve
Loose plug
Loose head

Runs clean, will not richen

Fuel vent blocked
Improper lubricant
Defective plug
Improper carb setting
Fuel line too small
Fuel line clogged
Air leak in tank
Air leak in line
Air leak in carb
Head screws loose
Loose case screws

Won't idle

Bad plug
Bad fuel
Loose carb
Wrong carb setting
Case screws loose
Head screws loose
Loose plug
Fuel line too large
Leak at carb base

Won't start

No fuel
Flooded
Dead battery
Defective plug
Bad fuel
Defective leads
Loose plug
Loose head
Improper connection
Wrong carb setting

Runs a short time and quits

Pick-up off in tank
Clogged filter
Clogged carb
Loose carb
Loose needle
Bad plug
Fuel line too large
Blocked vent

CHAPTER 6

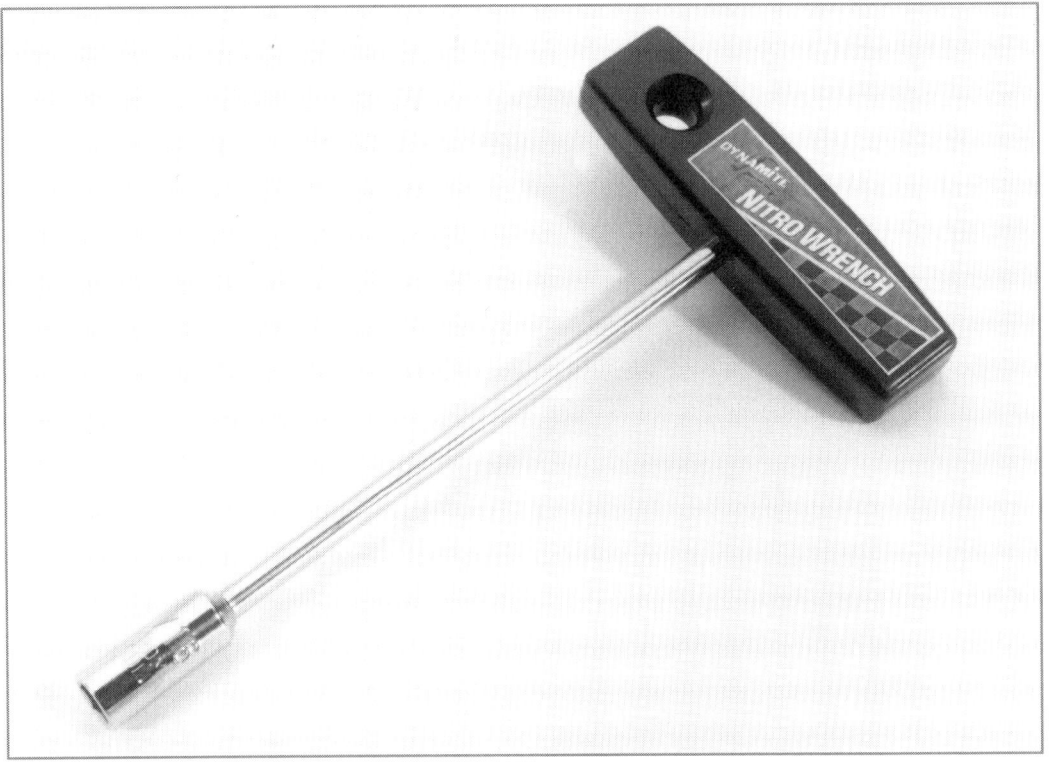

Above: Dynamite's nitro wrench for removing glow plugs. Left: DuraTrax's fuel bottle.

Thunder* and Byron* both make good fuel that's designed for car racing. Fuel comes with several percentages of nitro: 10, 20 and 30 percent. Most car racers use 20-per-cent-nitro fuel.

Pit Box Accessories

There are several things you should always have with you when you go out to run a gas car. Most people get some type of inexpensive tool caddy and pile all their stuff into it. A good pit box will contain your starter and a 12V battery; a glow-plug driver; spare plugs; fuel and a fuel bottle; and wrenches to remove plugs and tires.

Gas cars are a total blast! There's nothing like the sound and power you get from nitro-burnin' machines, but I suggest that you start with electric cars. There's enough to deal with with any R/C car, let alone a small, 2-stroke engine. Learn the basics, and after that, when you want to go all out, go gas!

CHAPTER 7

Basic Race Tuning

- Off-road tuning

- On-road tuning

- Shocks

- Wings and spoilers

- Tire selection

CHAPTER 7

It's impossible to say that there's just one correct setup for a particular R/C car because there are so many variables to deal with; track surface, temperature, size of obstacles and the length of the race should all be taken into account. And there are so many adjustments you can make to your car that it's best to follow this rule of thumb: build your car as the instructions indicate, and if you make changes, make only one at a time. People are often tempted to adjust three or four variables at once, and then they can't figure out which one actually caused the improvement—or the disaster! Before setting up your car, you could also ask the advice of an experienced racer at the track.

Off-Road

To make cars easier to control, most manufacturers have developed elaborate suspension systems, the most versatile of which is the four-wheel (4W) independent. With this, every wheel has its own

Measuring camber with RPM's camber gauge.

shock absorber, spring, control arms and adjustments.

The length of the control arm (the lower arm) isn't adjustable, but on some cars, you can adjust the rear toe-in. The upper link holds the wheels upright and, ultimately, adjusts the wheel's camber. Camber can be seen from the front and rear of a car. Get down to the car's level and look at it head-on. Do the tops of the wheels lean inward or outward? The number of degrees they lean is referred to as "camber," and you can alter it by adjusting

By adjusting the location of the upper link mount, you can cause camber to change as the suspension compresses (see photos A and B).

A.

B.

64 GETTING STARTED IN R/C CARS

BASIC RACE TUNING

Rear toe on the Losi Jr. series can be adjusted by changing rear arm blocks.

the length of the upper link. To make the camber change as the suspension moves, you can also adjust the upper link where it's attached at either end. Most car-kit instructions give you the settings for the initial construction, so stick to them.

On-Road

On-road cars usually have simpler suspension systems. Most have only ¼ inch of front-suspension travel and no damping. The rear end is usually attached to the chassis on a T-bar that allows the rear wheels to pivot left to right and front to back. The rear usually has a shock or two to handle the bumps and, sometimes, a friction damper as well.

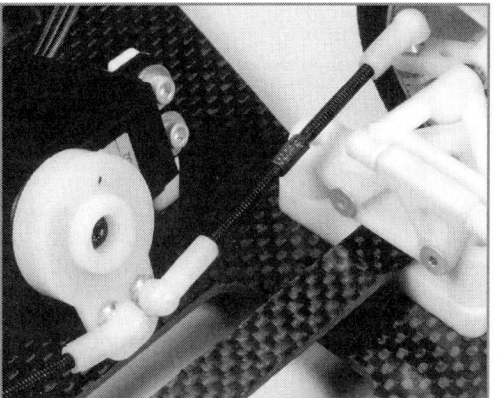
Associated's Dynamic Strut front suspension.

A friction damper is often a pair of plastic pucks that lightly sandwich the rear pod's upper plate. The pod's action can then be controlled by altering the pucks' tension and by adding a little silicone "goo." Generally speaking, the stiffer the rear suspension, the more steering you get; the looser the rear suspension, the less steering you get.

In the '90s, a new type of front suspension has started to show up at tracks. It's called a "Reactive Caster" or "Dynamic Strut" front end. The design allows the caster setting of the front end to vary during suspension travel if desired. This can make the steering much more aggressive, so it isn't for every application.

If you have a car with this type of front end, experiment with the caster settings until you find one that suits your driving

Very small springs provide a slight amount of front suspension on most on-road pan cars.

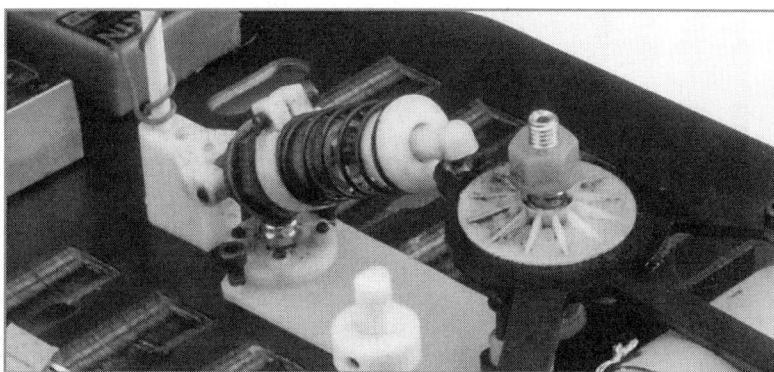
Rear suspension is handled by an oil filled coil-over on this Associated 10L. The damper pucks also control the rear pod action.

CHAPTER 7

style. Start with a setting for fixed caster, and see how your car handles. If you think you can use a bit more steering response, try the reactive setup.

Shocks

Shock absorbers are a necessity. If your full-size car didn't have them, you'd drive over a bump and still feel its effects five blocks away. On R/C cars, shocks allow you to travel over very rough terrain and still maintain control—even at high

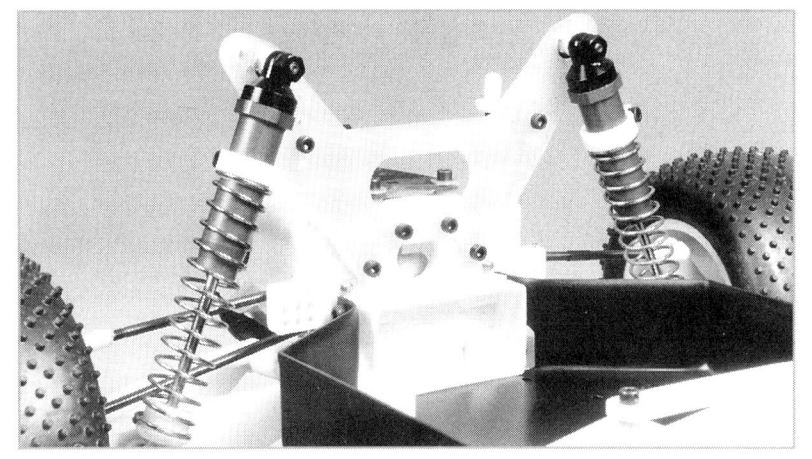

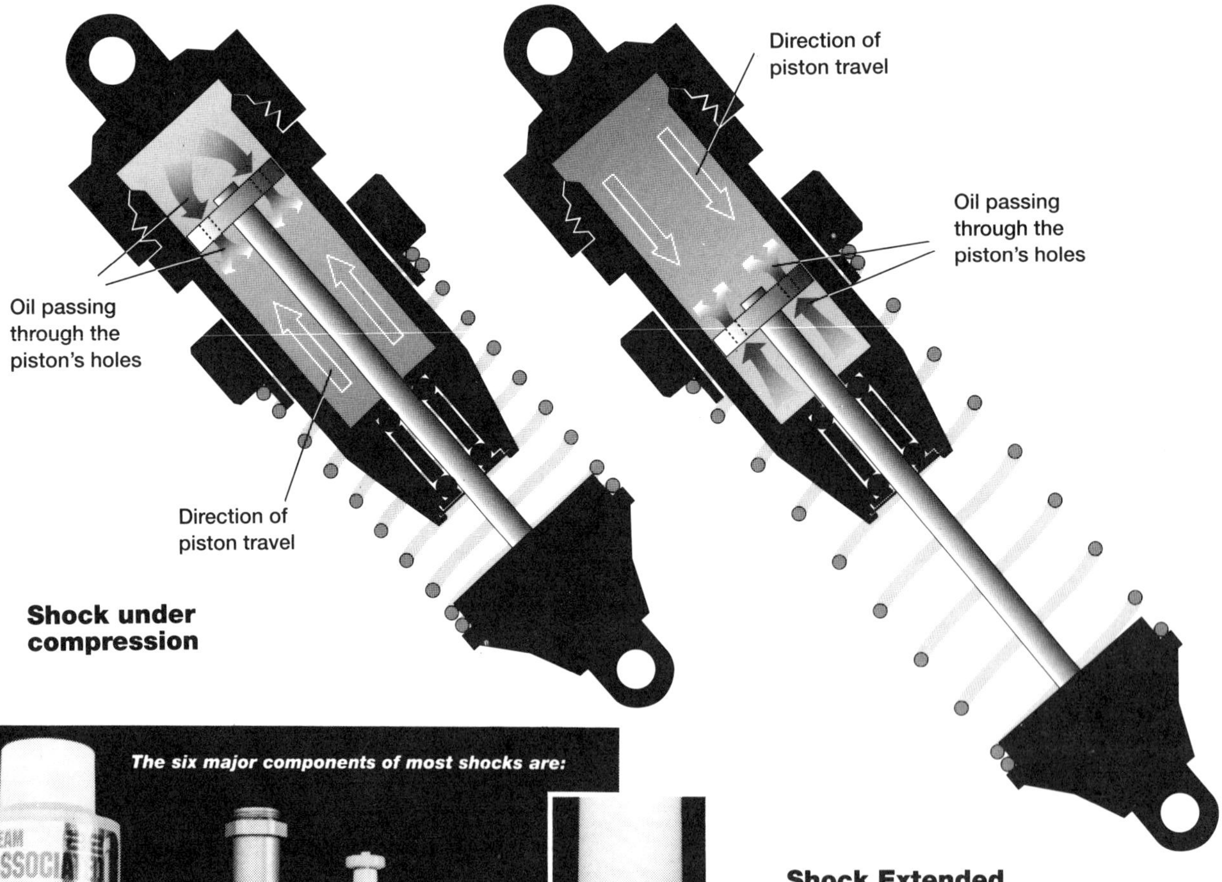

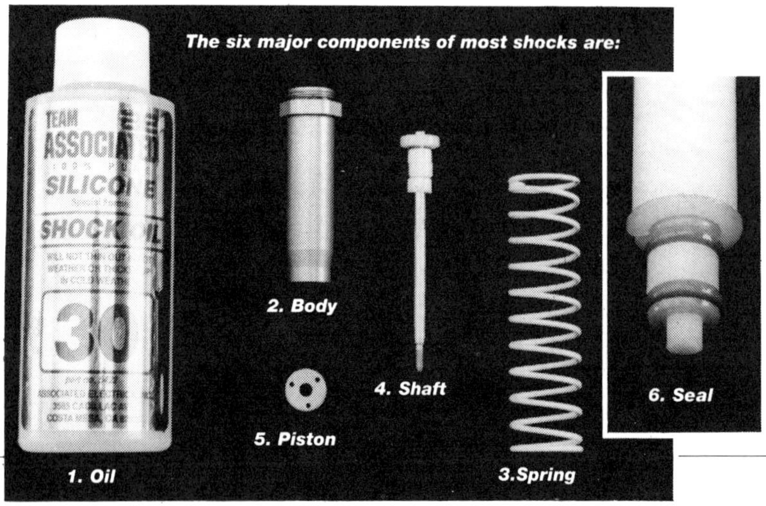

Shock under compression

Shock Extended

Oil passing through the piston's holes

Direction of piston travel

The six major components of most shocks are:

1. Oil
2. Body
3. Spring
4. Shaft
5. Piston
6. Seal

66 GETTING STARTED IN R/C CARS

BASIC RACE TUNING

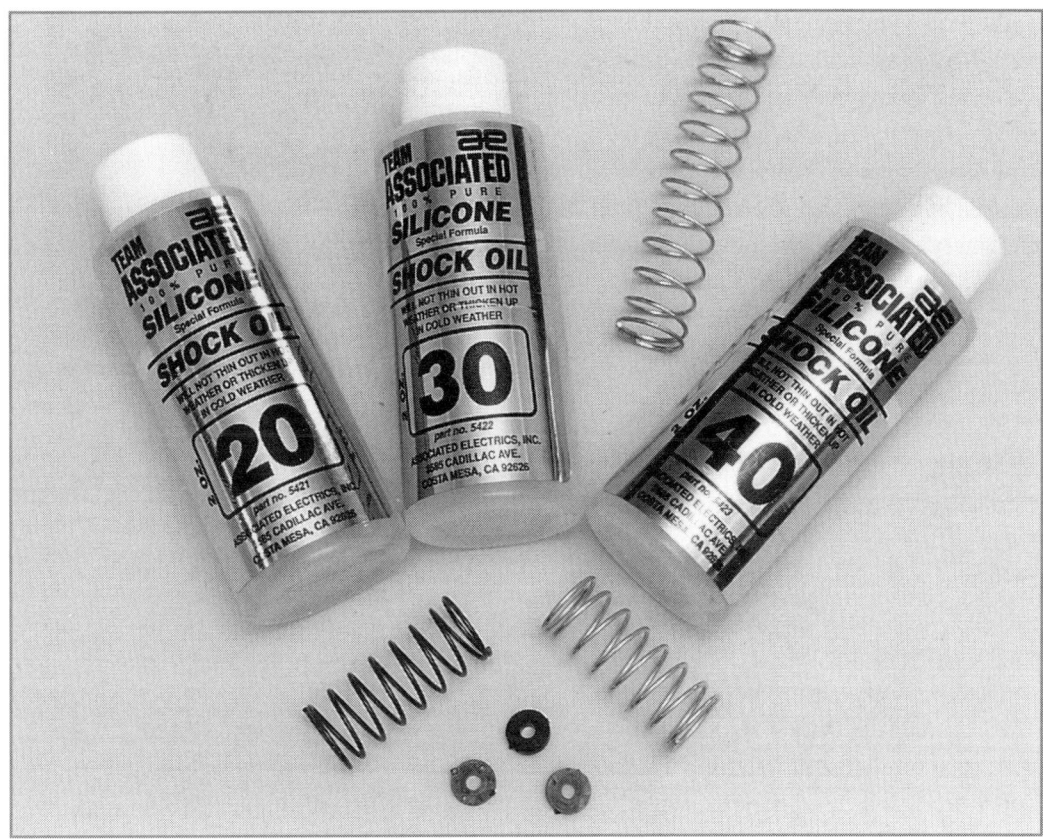
Shock oil, springs and oil all affect how your suspension works.

speeds. Most good shock absorbers are what we call oil-filled coil-overs because they're filled with oil and they have coil springs that go over the shock bodies.

Shock Oil

Shock oil is very important to the suspension. As the car's suspension is compressed, a piston on the end of the shock shaft travels through oil inside the shock body. Small holes or a notch in the piston allow oil to pass through the piston as it moves. The oil's thickness determines how quickly the piston can travel. A bumpy track will require shocks that work faster, so choose a thinner oil. On smooth tracks, you need a firmer suspension, so use a thicker oil. You may also use a thinner oil in just the front or the rear to increase traction in the end you need it.

Shock oil is classified by its weight—10 weight (WT), 20WT, 30WT and so on (not all manufacturers use the same numbers). To find the correct oil for your shocks, you need to have a selection of several weights and do some experimenting. Use a good-quality silicone oil, such as the ones sold by Team Losi, Trinity, and Associated. Silicone shock oil doesn't thicken in cold weather or thin out in the heat, so performance is consistent.

Just as the weight of the oil controls the rate of piston travel, so does the piston itself. The size of the piston's holes (or notches) and how many there are also determine how the suspension will work. Most of the kits that have oil-filled shocks come with a selection of pistons that have been graded with numbers or colors so that you can tell them apart. A piston with larger (or more) holes will allow oil to pass through more quickly and give less resistance (damping).

When you build oil-filled shocks, try to

CHAPTER 7

build them symmetrically. If you use 30WT oil in the right front shock, use it in the left front shock as well. Feel the action of both assembled shocks to see how they compare. When they're compressed, if one pushes the rod back out and the other doesn't, you need to work on one. Try to bleed a little oil out of it by loosening the cap and compressing the rod. Whatever you do, keep the shocks balanced.

Wings

"Do wings actually do anything on an R/C car?" is a common question. The answer is, without a doubt, yes! I've seen firsthand the effect a wing can have. In a carpet oval race, I ran a pan car that had a small Lexan wing with side dams. The side dams provided stability at high speeds, and the rest of the wing exerted downforce directly on the rear wheels. Well, during the race, another car and mine crashed, and my car lost its wing. I was marshalled well, and I was back on the track in a couple of seconds. I punched the throttle to bring the car back up to speed, but it was all over for me. As the car reached the next turn, it was very difficult for me to hold a straight line, and the car squirmed from side to side. When I started to turn, the car suddenly spun into the inner barrier, where

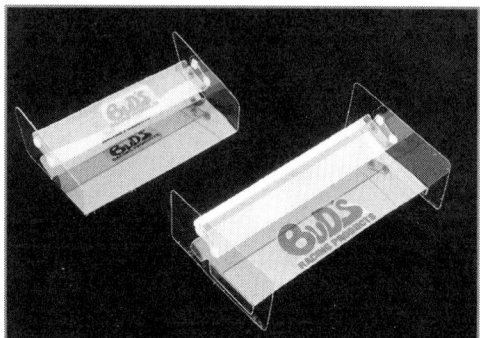

Wings are available in many shapes and sizes.

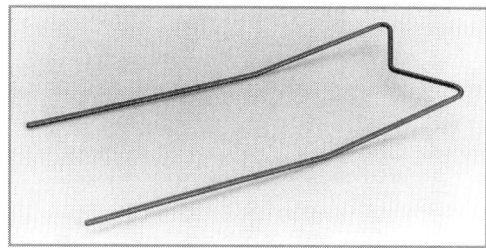

Wing wire can be bent to adjust downforce for a particular track.

it was promptly hit by another car. I tried to make a go of it one more time, but it was no use; the car needed that wing to be stable and to hold the rear end on the ground.

If you hold your hand out of the window of your full-size car (when it's moving at about 30mph), you can see the effect a wing has. If you hold your hand horizontal, you don't feel much effect from the wind. If you tilt the front edge of your hand downward, though, the downforce will be immediately apparent. On an R/C car, the wing is usually attached with flexible wire. This allows you to adjust the wing's angle to vary the downforce. Most wings are flat and curved or angled upward at the rear. Set them flat to begin with; you can tilt them to increase downforce if it's needed.

Spoilers

You can also affect your car's aerodynamics by installing a spoiler: a flat strip of Lexan that's attached to the tail of the car. Like a wing, it's designed to increase rear traction, but it does so in a slightly

Tecnacraft's* on/off-road wing.

68 GETTING STARTED IN R/C CARS

BASIC RACE TUNING

Spoilers like this one add downforce to the rear of the vehicle.

different way. Most racing trucks and some pan cars use spoilers.

In racing, the size of spoilers and wings is limited. Acceptable dimensions are specified in the rule books of each race organization, and most of the wings on the market meet the required specs.

Off-road cars take more abuse, so, in many cases, a Lexan wing isn't strong enough. For off-road, you might want to try a molded-plastic wing. Plastic is more flexible than Lexan, so your wing will bounce back into shape after a hard hit.

Tire Selection

How your vehicle handles has a lot to do with the tires you choose. Believe it or not, your tires are more important than your batteries, your motor, or even your radio system. Let's face it: your car can have all the power in the world, but if your tires don't grip, you can't use it. Tires vary in width, tread pattern, what they're made of (compound, or rubber formula) and profile (height of the tire compared with the

Losi X-pattern tires.

CHAPTER 7

Typical mini-pin for hard tracks.

Step-pins for medium to hard tracks.

Spikes for softer tracks.

rim diameter). All these will affect the way the tire grips the pavement and the dirt.

• **Off-road.** Off-road tires usually have a very aggressive tread pattern that consists of spikes and/or bars. The number of spikes, their arrangement and the tire compound used will all determine how much traction a given tire will have. Generally speaking, the harder the track is, the softer the tires and the smaller (shorter) the spikes should be; the softer the track is, the harder the tires and the larger (longer) the spikes should be.

On a very hard track, large spikes tend to fold over under acceleration, so many drivers trim them down, with clippers or small scissors, into short stubby spikes.

You can vary tire traction to find the correct balance between oversteering and understeering. Let's say you run a 2WD buggy, and it spins out whenever you try to make a turn. This is known as oversteering. The spin-out occurs because there's more traction on the front wheels than on the rear wheels. The first thing you should try is to increase rear-tire traction. Switching to a tire made of a softer compound or to one with smaller spikes might do the trick.

Though softer tires provide more traction, some are so soft that they don't hold

BASIC RACE TUNING

A tire truer grinds a rough-cut foam tire to the right diameter.

their shape well and need the support of soft, foam, donut-shaped inserts. The inserts will help the tires to keep their shape.

• **On-road.** On-road tires are usually made of foam rubber. A foam "donut" is glued to the rim and is then trued down to the proper diameter on a tire truer (a motor that spins the wheel at high speed and has attachments with which you can trim or sand the foam to a specific size).

Use tires made of different compounds to increase or decrease traction. Different compounds are denoted by dots of various colors that you'll find on the tires' rims.

• **Green-dot**—standard tires that are included in most pan-car kits.

• **Yellow-dot**—a softer compound that offers much better traction.

• **Blue-dot**—harder and lasts longer. Experimentation will help you choose a compound that wears well and offers good traction. There are other, more "exotic" compounds, such as purple-, gold- and silver-dot, but they're more expensive and usually used for gas racing.

For better traction and longer life, treat your foam tires with traction compound. It doesn't make the tires sticky; instead, it conditions the foam to make it more supple. This will increase traction and will help to prevent the tires from drying out. When you decide to apply tire compound,

Some donuts come pre-trued and ready for mounting on a rim.

CHAPTER 7

Traction compound is great for adding traction to foam tires.

start with the rears. If the increased rear traction reduces the front traction to a point at which turning is difficult, apply compound to the fronts as well. Start by coating half of the tire; apply more compound if you need even more steering.

Final Points to Remember

• Keep good notes on how your car is set up.
• When tuning, make only one change at a time. It's easy to go overboard, try several things at once and get lost in your settings.
• Note the effect a change has on the car's handling.
• Note the temperature and which types of tire and motor you're using. The better your notes, the more help they'll be to you in the future.

CHAPTER 8

Building, Painting and Detailing your Model

- Deciphering the instructions

- Building tips

- Cutting and trimming Lexan

- Masking

- Paint and decals

CHAPTER 8

How well you build and finish your model is what sets it apart from the thousands of others in the world. The key rule to follow? Take your time. Don't rush, or you'll regret it later. In this chapter, I'll tell you which supplies you'll need and how you can finish your vehicle so it looks great.

Deciphering the Instructions

Every kit comes with an instruction book. Some are good, and some...well, let's just say they're not so good. With others, you often just need to study them a bit to fig-

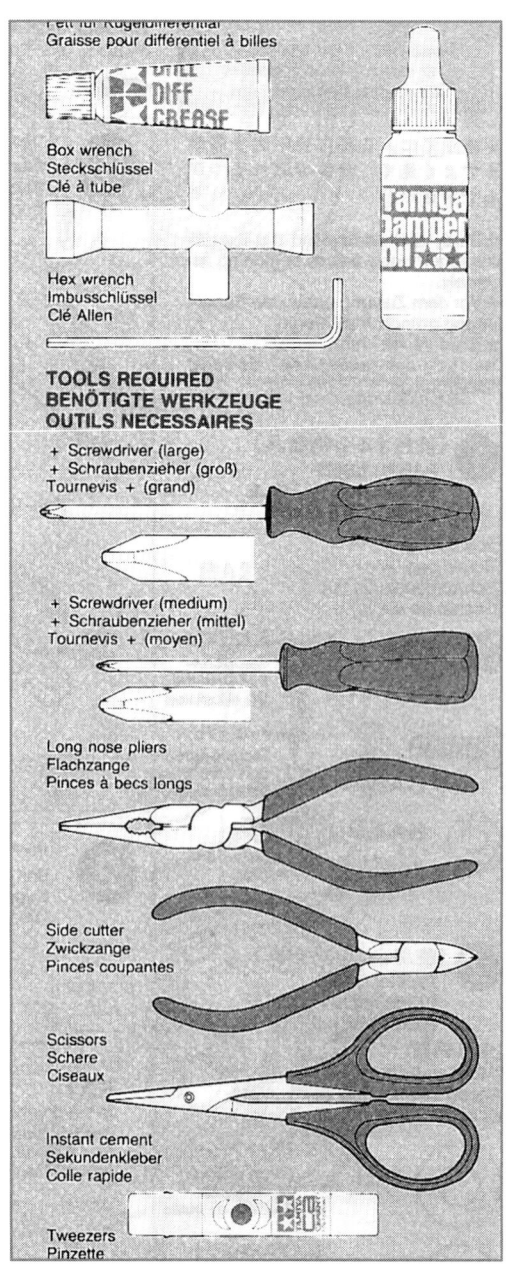

Most good instructions will list all the tools and components needed to complete the kit.

74 GETTING STARTED IN R/C CARS

ure them out. In the beginning of the booklet, most list the tools you'll need. If the instructions use diagrams rather than photos, there will usually be little figures and icons to look for. For example, Tamiya uses a little tube icon to mark a part that needs to be lubricated. A similar icon is used for thread-lock, so make sure you know the difference!

Most instructions give full-size pictures of the hardware needed for each step. Double-check each part to ensure that you have the right one. Some screws have fine threads and some are self-tapping, so they cut their own threads; be sure you know the difference.

Rule number one: always start from the beginning! The steps are in an order for a reason, so stick to them. OK, you can put a tire on a rim to check it out, but don't go any further than that.

Hints

The easiest—and worst—thing you can do is to lose track of hardware. I've found that using a number of zip-lock bags makes building easier. Say a kit comes with bags marked "A" through "F." Pull the header off each bag, and put it and the contents of the bag into a zip-lock bag. When you need screw E2, you can just look for the zip-lock with the "E" header in it and

A muffin tin or zip-lock bag is a great way to keep parts separated during assembly.

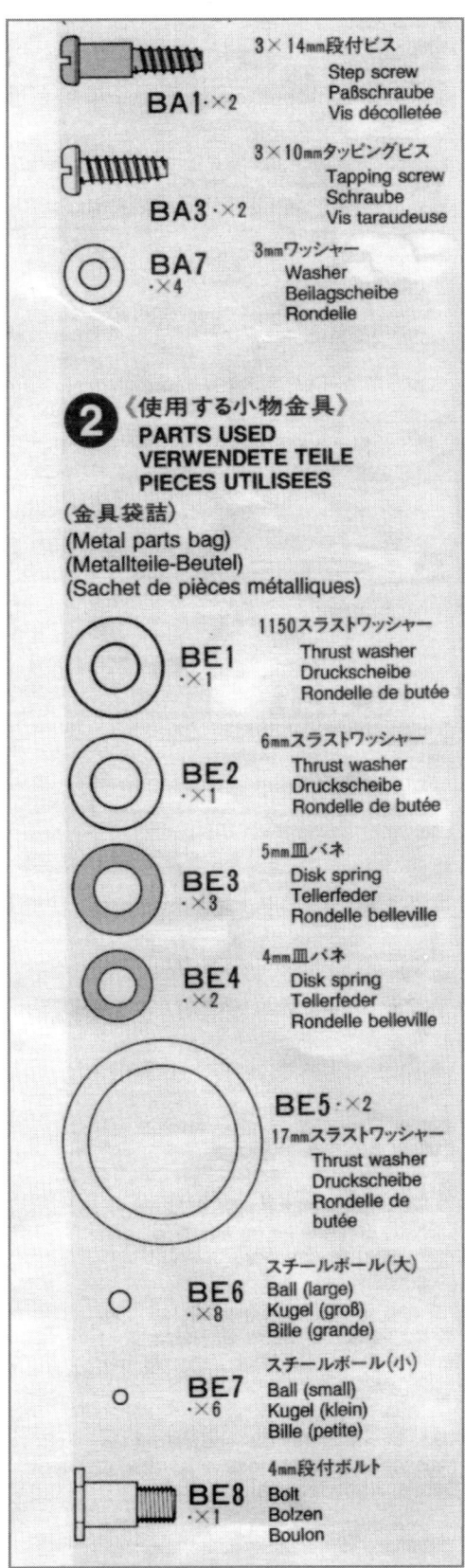

A good set of instructions will have diagrams that show the parts needed for each step.

CHAPTER 8

Trim the nubs off plastic parts with a sharp X-Acto knife.

find the screw easily. You can also use a muffin tin to hold the contents of a number of bags, but it's very easy to knock it over and mix everything up.

If there are molded parts in the kit, make sure that you trim all the rough scrap spots off each one. Many parts are molded with many other parts in what is called a "tree." Several little "branches" connect the various parts together so the plastic can flow to all of them. When the parts are broken off the tree, there are usually small bumps and nubs left on them; these should be removed with a sharp hobby knife.

As you assemble the suspension and steering components, make sure they operate freely. It's sometimes necessary to trim a part to make it work correctly. If there's too much play on, say, a suspension arm, use shims between the block and arm to reduce it.

Thread-lock

The number-one rule for gas cars is use thread-lock! The vibrations caused by a gas engine will shake your car back into kit form if you don't take precautions. Bolts threaded into plastic parts don't need thread-lock, but bolts threaded into metal parts do. If you have nylon nuts or nuts with nylon inserts in one end, they're safe, but if they're just plain metal nuts, use thread-lock.

Loctite makes two types of thread-lock that I recommend you use. One is no. 271 (red) and the other is no. 242 (blue). Blue

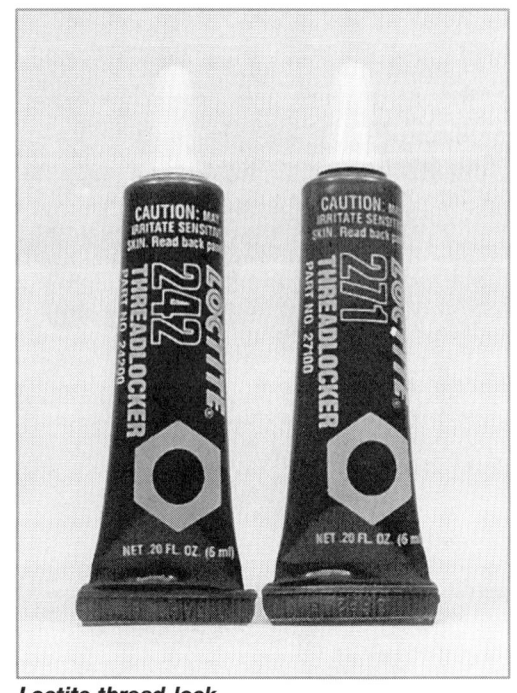

Loctite thread-lock.

Building, Painting and Detailing Your Model

is for medium-strength connections that you want to be able to remove easily. The red stuff is very strong and should be used only on large bolts, such as engine-mount bolts, that you won't remove very often. To make removal easier, you can heat parts with a lighter or a small torch, but be sure that you don't melt any of the surrounding plastic parts.

Cutting and Trimming Lexan Bodies

Lexan (polycarbonate) bodies have revolutionized our hobby. They're extremely light and strong, and they look great. You paint them on the inside, so the paint is protected. These bodies are, however, tricky to trim correctly. Most of the bodies included with kits from Tamiya and Kyosho come trimmed, and the mounting holes have been drilled. Some people like to cut and trim a body before they paint it; others like to do it afterward; either way works.

If you decide to paint first, before you start, it's a good idea to mark where you'll drill the mounting holes. Set the body on the chassis and center it over the wheels.

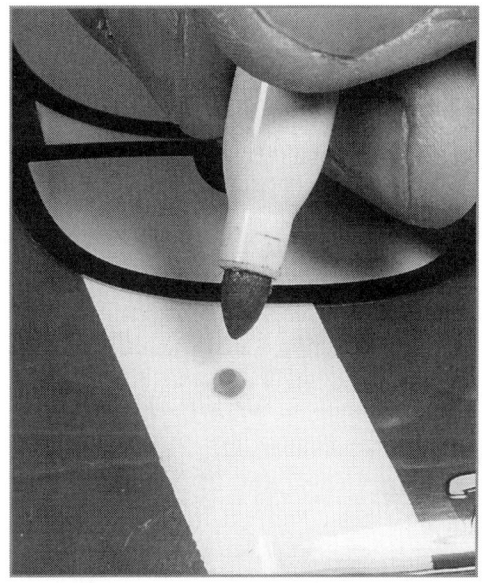

Mark holes to be drilled with a Sharpie marker. Extra marks can be removed with alcohol.

Use a Sharpie marker to make little marks over the tips of the body-mounting posts. You can wipe them off later with alcohol.

On some cars, the wheel-well openings are clearly marked and easy to cut out; on some, they're not marked, so you can cut them to fit your particular wheelbase. If they aren't marked, find a spray can that's slightly larger than the wheel, and use its base as a template. You can draw all over

Use a paint can to mark wheel openings on a body.

CHAPTER 8

Using the "pizza" cutting method to remove the parts for the opening.

I start a hole by piercing the body with an X-Acto knife and twisting.

the outside of the body and wipe it off later, so make all the marks you need to get the wheel well lined up correctly. I usually mark the center line of the wheel vertically and then figure how far up from the edge of the body I want the top of the well to be. Measure both sides in the same way, and then draw a circle with the can as a guide. If you're satisfied, duplicate it on the other side; if you aren't, wipe the marks off.

To cut the circle out, I use the "pizza" method. With a sharp X-Acto knife, scribe a line on the circle you drew before. Be careful not to slip; you don't need much force. Cut with scissors from the bottom edge of the body to very close to the circle you just scribed. Cut several pizza-shaped slices. After that, you can just fold the pieces inward and get them to bend on the scribed line. At the scribed line, the Lexan will break away cleanly and easily. Continue this with the other pieces, and then use light sandpaper to smooth the cut edge if necessary.

There are a couple of ways to drill the holes for your body posts. One way is with an electric drill and a bit of the correct size. This works, but it's very easy for the bit to wander and drill a hole off-center. I use an X-Acto knife to start a hole and then use a tapered reamer to enlarge it to the correct size. I then trim any extra flashing away with the knife.

You can cut long, straight pieces of the body with either a pair of scissors or an X-Acto knife. With scissors, just cut straight and evenly along your line. It's easier to make a straight cut if you lay a piece of tape along the line. If you use an X-Acto knife, use tape or a ruler as a guide to scribe a straight line. Then simply fold the Lexan along the line to break the piece off.

For curved areas of the body, you can use either a curved pair of scissors or an X-Acto knife. Be very careful using an

Building, Painting and Detailing Your Model

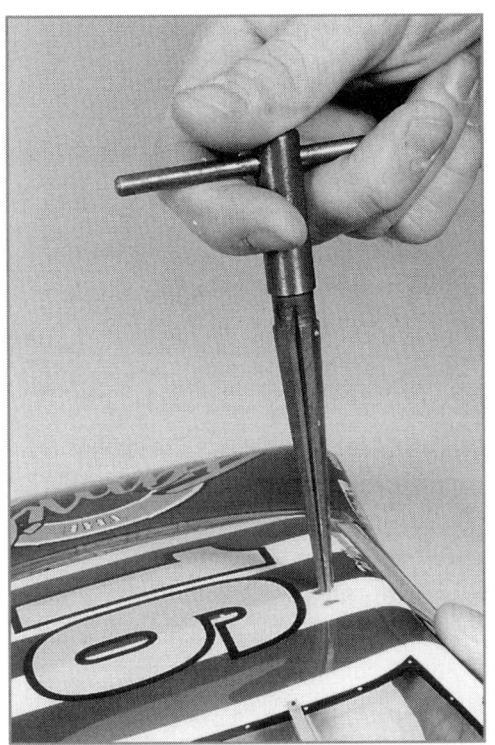

A tapered reamer will enlarge the hole to the desired size.

X-Acto knife on curved parts of a body; it's very easy to slip and ruin your new body—or a finger. In some tricky areas, it helps to use a Dremel tool with a sanding drum.

Masking

Whether you trimmed your body or not, if you're ready to paint, you must first mask. As with everything else, there's more than one way to do it. The most simple method is with masking tape. I usually start by covering the outside of the body with newspaper or the bag the body came in. If there are holes drilled in the body, use small pieces of tape to seal them.

Decide which type of design you want and which colors you want to use. Start with the darkest colors and finish with the lightest. Say you want a white body with a heavy blue line down the center. Start by masking every part that you want to paint white. You'll end up with a heavy clear section down the center of the hood. Paint it with several light coats of blue, letting it dry between each coat. Let it dry completely overnight, then remove the masking and paint the rest white. If you painted the white first, the blue would darken it.

Another way to mask is with liquid masking film. It's liquid latex rubber, and when it's dry, you can cut intricate designs in it. The best way to apply liquid mask is with a big brush. Just slop a big glob of it into the body and paint every nook and cranny. Make sure you don't feather any edges, or it will be difficult to peel off later. The thicker the coating of rubber is, the better. If the masking film you bought is thin, you might need a couple of coats. I accelerate drying with a warm lamp or a hair dryer. (Make sure the body doesn't get too hot, or it could become deformed.)

When the liquid mask is dry, it's almost perfectly clear. If there are any areas that look milky white, let it dry longer. If you think the coating isn't thick enough, add another coat. The thicker the coating is, the easier it will be to remove later.

One of the coolest things about liquid mask is that you can draw on it with a

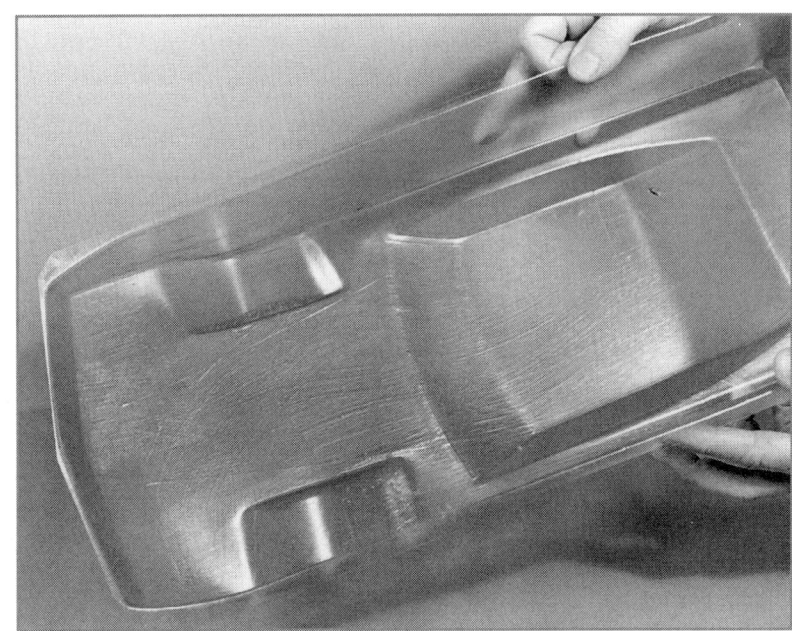

A generous coating of liquid mask dries almost perfectly clear.

GETTING STARTED IN R/C CARS 79

CHAPTER 8

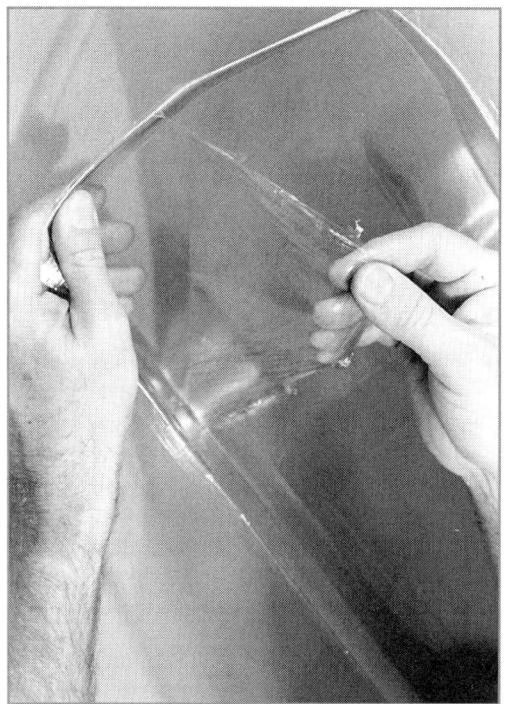

After drawing and cutting a design, the liquid mask can be removed so that you can paint a section.

sharp X-Acto knife to cut along the lines. Say you're painting a car with flames on the front edge of the hood. First remove all of the mask for the main body color, leaving only the flames and windows covered. Apply the main color, and let it dry. Then just remove the flames and paint the body with red, yellow and white. Liquid mask makes very sharp, well-defined lines.

Paint

You should always use paint designed specifically for polycarbonate bodies. (You can find it in most hobby shops.) Pactra* R/C Finish (see picture below) is probably the most common. Most colors need no explanation: you just spray them on. Some require a bit more work. Metallic paint should be applied in light coats and then backed with silver or gold paint. This helps the metallic effect come out correctly. Fluorescent paints should be applied in light coats as well, but backed with white.

ballpoint pen. If you want flames, just draw them on paper, hold the paper on the outside of the body and hold the body up to a light. Then simply trace the lines onto the mask with a pen. Once you have a design mapped out on the mask, use a

Paints are sold in jars for brushing or for use in airbrushes, and in spray cans. You can apply jar paint with a brush with

Make sure the paint you use was designed for Lexan bodies, or it won't adhere correctly.

80 GETTING STARTED IN R/C CARS

Building, Painting and Detailing Your Model

Trim your decals to size and trim a small section of the backing. Now you can position the decal and be sure it's straight.

great results, because the body provides the finishing gloss. Even if there are huge brush strokes on the inside, it still looks smooth and even on the outside. The only time you can't use a brush is with metallic paint. To get the best results, the small metal particles have to be sprayed; a brush will spread them unevenly.

Decals

Decals add that extra bit of flair to any R/C car. Most car kits include decals; the rest leave it up to you. Regardless, make sure you trim and apply them with care. If you have individual decals with backing, peel a small section of the backing away and cut it off. Then you can position the

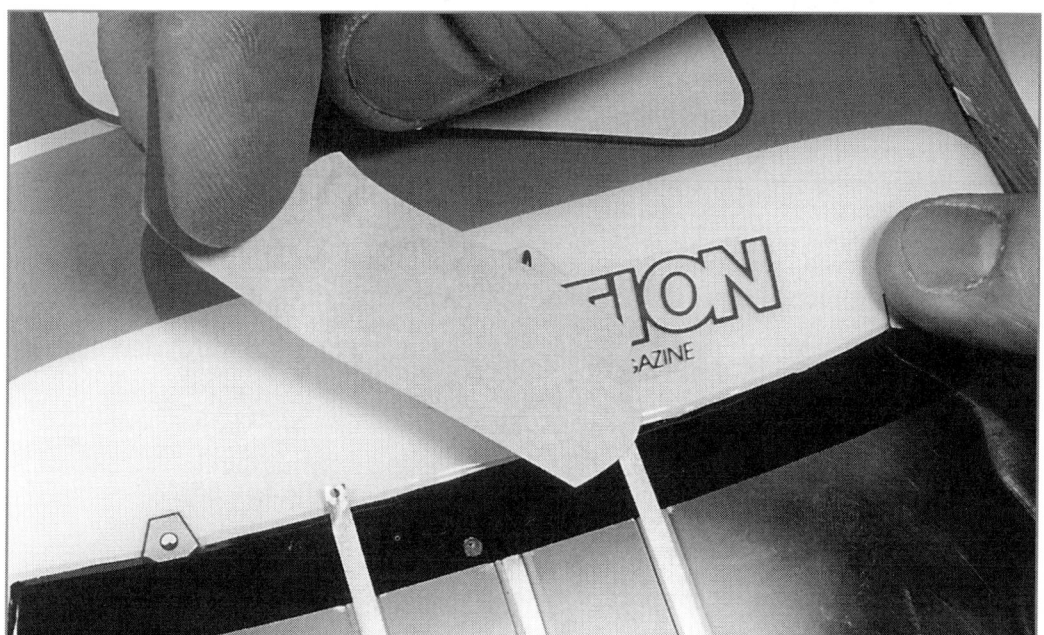
Next, gently remove the rest of the backing and rub the decal to secure it.

This body is finished with two colors of paint and about 100 decals.

decal easily and tack it into place when you're satisfied with its placement. Remove the rest of the backing and smooth the decal out. I use a credit card to smooth the decal from one side to the other to remove all the air bubbles.

If you have a large decal sheet with several small decals printed on it, you'll have to cut them out. You can either cut them with scissors and treat them like the decals already discussed, or you can carefully trim and place them with a sharp X-Acto knife.

Take your time, and you'll end up with a car that you'll be proud to own and race. Your first car might not end up looking like a work of art, but with time, you'll learn to get it right.

CHAPTER 9

Modifications and Hop-Ups

- Ball bearings

- Turnbuckles

- ESCs

- Modified motors

- Heat sinks

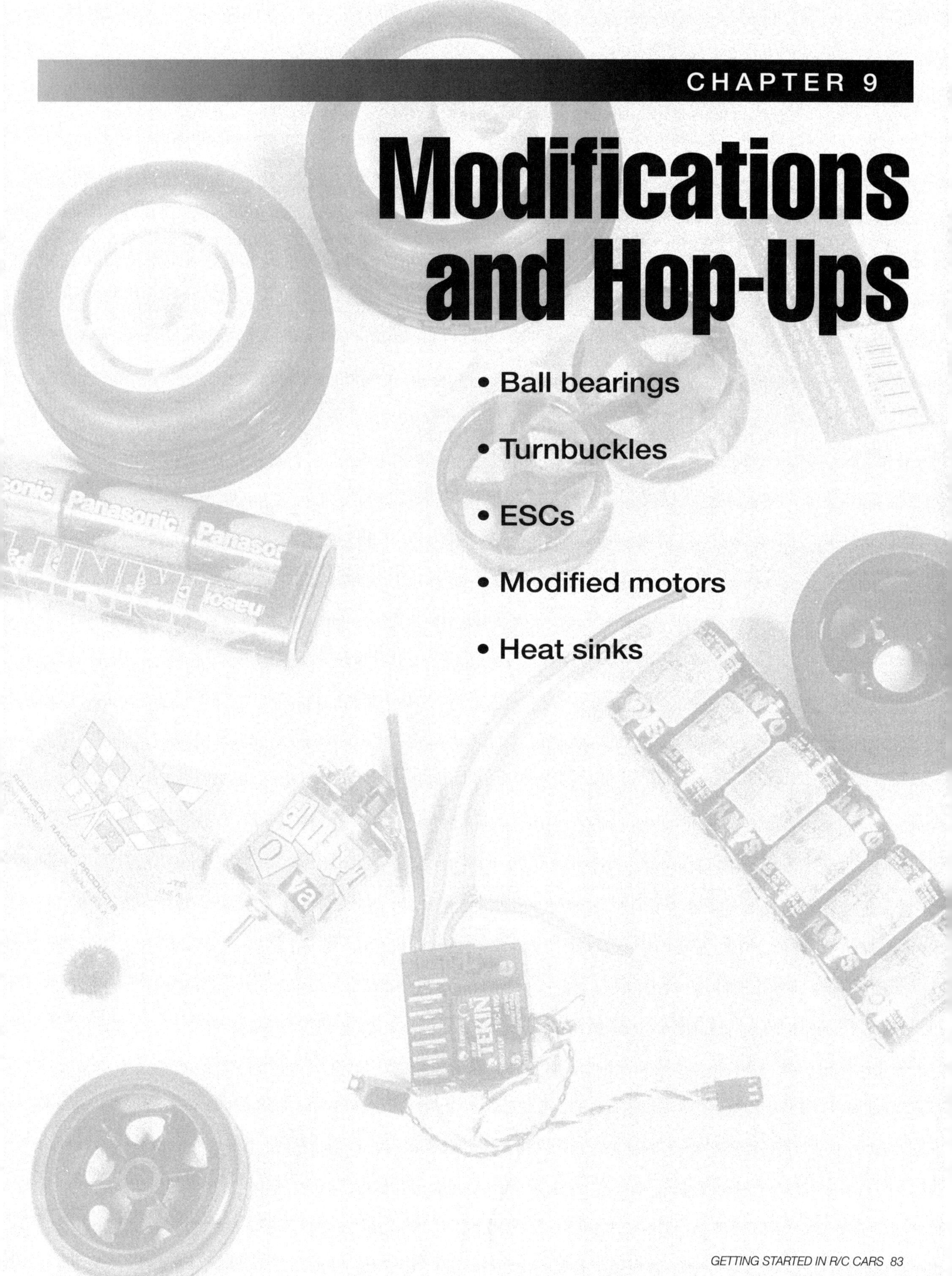

One of the best things about R/C cars is that you can change what you don't like. If your car keeps popping a steering linkage, you can get stronger rod ends. If your steering system is tight or sloppy, you can buy a ball-bearing version that's as smooth as silk. But be warned: it's easy to get carried away! Don't go out and buy something just because it looks cool; buy it only if it will solve a real problem.

Electric and Gas

• **Ball bearings.** One of the best ways to modify your car is by installing a good set of ball bearings. In many kits, metal or plastic bushings are included for all the rotating parts. They're much less expensive than bearings, so they keep the kit's price down. After many hours of use, however, they'll start to wear out and become sloppy. You should be able to find a kit for your car that will have all the bearings you need. You can also buy bearings individually, but this usually costs more. Wheels that used to wobble and shake will run smooth and true with bearings, and overall performance will improve. Run times will increase slightly, as will top speed.

• **Tires.** Next, I'd invest in another set of tires. If you have a car that was designed for off-road use, get a set of tires and rims that are strictly for on-road use. Then you can save the spiked set that came with the car for the dirt. If the stock tires are already worn out because of pavement driving, get a set of new off-road tires.

A bearing kit contains a complete set for your particular car.

You can never have enough tires for your car.

Hop-Ups and Modifications

A good set of oil-filled shocks will dramatically improve the handling of any car.

• **Oil-filled shocks**. If your car doesn't have oil-filled shocks, this is a very good place to invest a few bucks. A good set of oil shocks will smooth out the bumps and give you much greater control. Check your manual to see whether a set is made for your car. If none is listed, go to your hobby shop and see what they can do. Chances are, there's a way to fit a set of shocks on your car.

• **Turnbuckles.** For a simple, inexpensive modification, add a set of turnbuckles. When you have a set of turnbuckles, it's easy to adjust toe-in, caster and camber. Most kits come with steering and suspension rods that are threaded in one direction. This means you have to pop off one end of the link to change its length and adjust the camber or toe-in. A turnbuckle has left-hand threads on one end and right-hand threads on the other. Once installed, you can adjust its length with a small

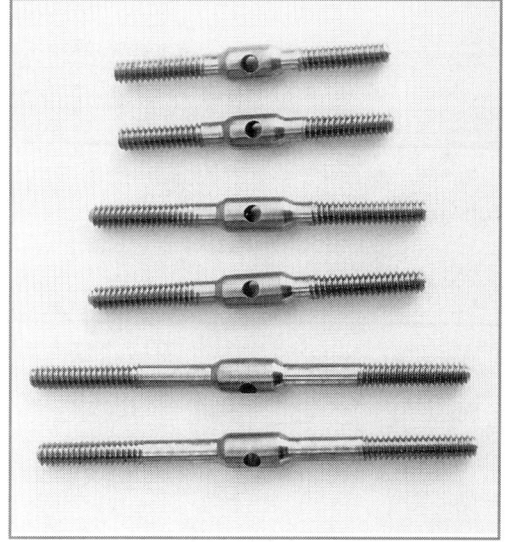

Turnbuckles make adjusting camber and toe-in easy.

wrench without having to remove anything. You can find universal steel turnbuckles for a couple of bucks and cut them to the correct length, or you can buy stronger, lighter, titanium turnbuckles.

They're a bit more expensive, and you must buy them in the correct length; but complete titanium kits are available for most cars.

Just for Electric

Most entry-level car kits come with mechanical speed controls. When they're new, they work well, but after a while, they start to develop "dead spots," which will cause the car's motor to stop. You can clean the dead spots, but they'll eventually wear out. If you want to make your throttle response 10 times better, invest in an electronic speed control (ESC). This small device electronically varies the power that's delivered to your motor. It has no moving parts to wear out, and it's much faster than a servo-controlled mechanical speed control. A mechanical unit takes time to shift from stop to full speed; an ESC does it instantly. An ESC also delivers current to your receiver and steering servo, so you don't need the stock onboard radio battery. An ESC replaces the throttle servo, the stock speed control, a bunch of wires and, in many cases, the receiver battery pack. A range of ESCs are available, from sport models for mild motors to super heavy-duty models for insane motors. Think about your plans when you buy an ESC. Don't buy a sport model if you want to get a faster motor in the future.

Most racing-type ESCs are forward only with brakes. This means that they control forward speed and brakes; no reverse is possible. This is the most efficient type of ESC, and it's great for fast vehicles. But for monster trucks, you might want reverse so that you can back away from that tree! There are special models with that capability. Check the features to be sure you know what you're buying: some reversing ESCs have proportional reverse; others have just an "emergency" reverse that blasts full speed to get you out of a jam.

If you have an electric car, you can always use another battery pack. The more

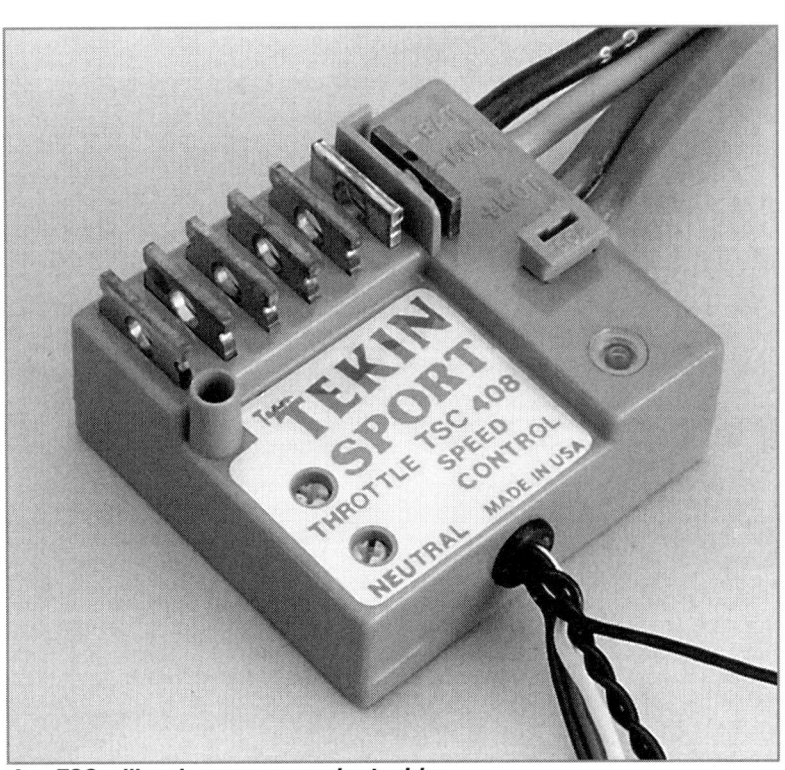

Any ESC will make your car easier to drive.

Batteries are another thing you can never have enough of.

Hop-Ups and Modifications

A modified motor will make your car much faster.

you have, the longer you can run without charging. I recommend that you get packs of 1400 SCR cells or 1700 SCRC cells. The SCRs are relatively inexpensive and are extremely durable. The SCRC cells are also very durable, but they're a little more expensive, owing to their higher capacity (longer run times).

If you want more speed, you need a faster motor. Most kits come with what's called a stock motor. A stock motor has bushings rather than bearings and it's usually wound so that it's mildly powered.

For your first modified motor, don't get something too crazy, or you'll destroy your gearbox and your run times. Start with a budget modified that has no fewer than 16 turns. You'll notice a great improvement in speed and acceleration, and you'll still get good run times. You can go down to 14- or 13-turn motors, but your run times will suffer.

Just for Gas

If you have a model that came with a CZ-R engine, the first thing you should

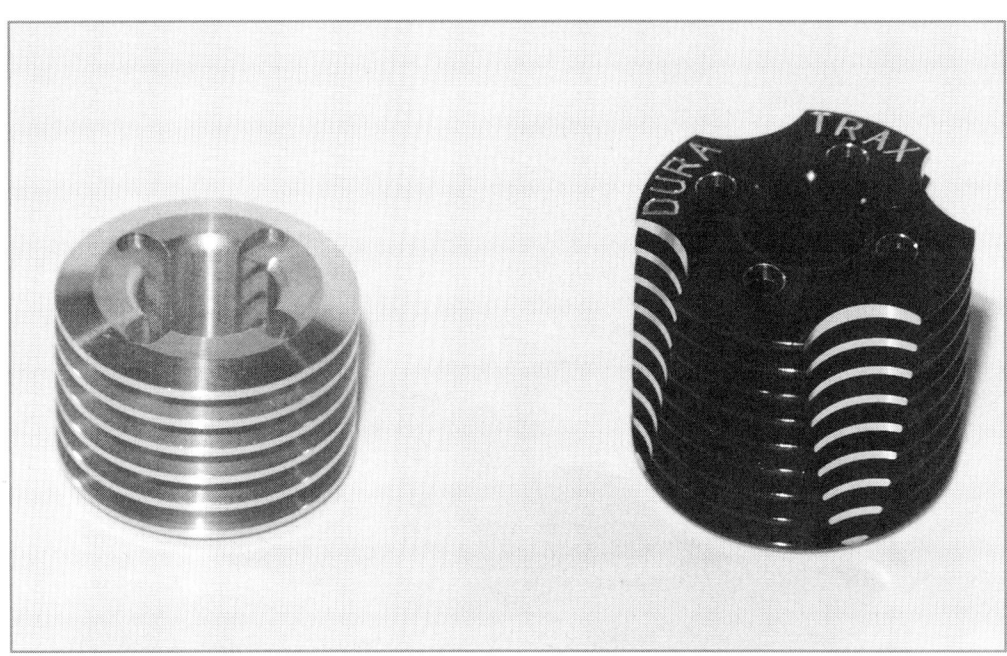

A heat-sink head will allow your engine to run cooler.

Always be sure you have a few spare glow plugs.

consider is a good heat-sink head. The stock head doesn't provide enough cooling for the best performance. With an aftermarket head, your engine will run cooler and last longer.

Although they aren't really mods, get a bunch of spare glow plugs. I like McCoy MC-59s for .12 engines and MC-9s or 8s for .21 engines.

Try to keep sight of your goals, and modify accordingly. Upgrade to a better part only if you have a legitimate problem with the stock part. It's easy to go overboard with trick-looking parts, but they might have a bigger effect on your wallet than on your car!

CHAPTER 10

Troubleshooting

- Answers to perplexing problems, from the pages of *Radio Control Car Action*.

CHAPTER 10

Rip It To Shreds

I have a Novak ESC. The other day, I bought new gears and motor brushes for my Ultima. I put all of the new stuff in my car, and it wouldn't run. I don't know what happened! I checked out the fuse, and that was OK; then I took the ESC apart and put it back together again. Still nothing. Can you help me?
John Montgomery
Milton, FL

If the problem started after you installed the new gears and motor brushes, then I doubt that it has anything do with the ESC. I can almost guarantee that it's the brushes. First, make sure that the lights on the ESC are functioning. If they aren't responding, then you have an ESC or battery-connection problem. If they're working, then check your motor. If you had to replace the brushes, chances are the commutator also needs some attention. Slide one of the brushes out of the motor, and look at the comm. If it's black and dirty, get a comm stick, and give it a few turns. This should do the trick if the motor is still in decent shape. Also, make sure that the brushes are free in the hoods by pulling on the brush wire and letting the brushes snap back against the comm.

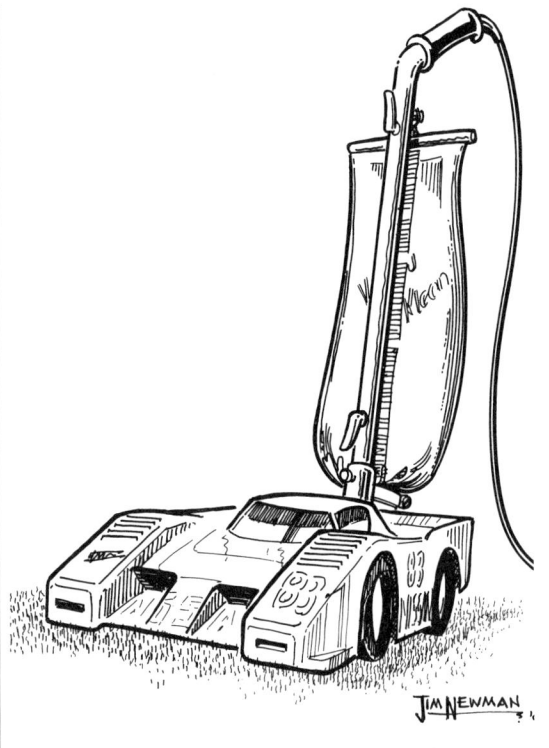

Carpet Fresh

I've been R/C racing for a year. I have a Cox .049 GTP Nissan, and I'm using the Sidewinder radio and the electronics that came with it. I was wondering if I could convert it for carpet racing and if I could use a .10 engine with the motor mount that came with it. Thank you for your help.
Adam Grube
Nazareth, PA

Unless you have some place outdoors to run on carpet, I wouldn't bother. The Cox .049 could be run on carpet right now, but the exhaust fumes will be a problem inside. As for the .10 engine—no dice! The mounts are completely different, and the engine is way too big to fit in the car. I'd stick with the .049 engine; it provides a lot of speed and power. If you want to go even faster, consider upgrading to a car like the Apex 10, or use a similar conversion for the Associated 10L.

Troubleshooting

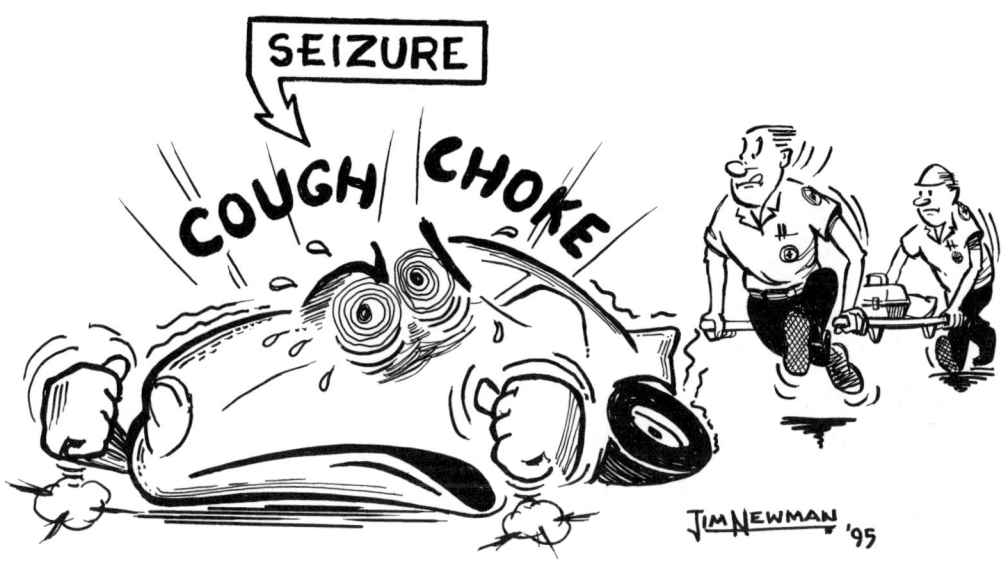

Seize the Day

I have a Porsche 911 with an O.S. .10 engine. I have trouble with the engine; it seems to seize when I try to start it up the second time. It un-seizes after 30 minutes; then it seems fine. Please help.
Billy Wulfken
Warrensburg, NY

The seizing you're experiencing is caused by too much fuel in your engine, otherwise known as flooding. When fuel is in the crankcase, it's drawn up into the combustion chamber and can't be compressed by the rising piston as a fuel/air mixture can. To remedy this, simply remove the glow plug, invert the car, and pull the starter cord a few times until all the fuel pours out. If it keeps happening, the mixture might be too rich. Try leaning in the needle a little, and see if that helps.

Grind-O-Rama

My Blackfoot truck keeps on grinding from the transmission but, if I remove the dogbones, it sounds OK. I can't find any broken or stripped teeth. I have no instructions, and there are no hobby shops close by, so I'd be grateful for your help.
Chris Von Roch
Omak, WA

You're headed in the right direction. The grinding sound is coming from the dogbones. On the Blackfoot, the dogbone has hexes on the ends that key into the tranny and the axles. The hexes wear out quickly, and they don't work as well as dogbones that have a ball with a crosspin-shaped end. I remember when I had a Blackfoot, I would go through a set of dogbones in one day (I took seven sets of replacements on my vacation).

You can lower the rear suspension to make the bones more level so they last longer, or you can replace the entire drive system with a kit made by Thorp that includes a ball diff, a counter gear and crosspin-type dogbones.

CHAPTER 10

The Nitty Gritty

I hope you can help me with this small problem. I recently purchased a set of ball bearings, and I've run my car out in the dirt several times since I installed them. I just took them out the other day, and they're feeling a little bit gritty. They aren't shot, are they? Do I have to buy new ones? I'm wondering if I can clean them out, and, if so, what's the proper way to do it? I don't want to ruin them.
FRANK REMICK
Brooklawn, NJ

If they feel gritty, you need to take care of them before it's too late. One method that works pretty well is to just blast them with motor spray and hope that all the bad stuff comes out. I jam the bearing on a tapered reamer, hold the bearing's outer race and give the reamer a good spin while I spray the cleaner. As long as you can get the spray into the bearing's shield, you should be able to get the gunk out.

If they still feel as if they need help, remove the shield. You'll need a good set of eyeballs and a knife that has a very fine tip. Not all bearing shields can be removed; the removable type has a tiny circular clip that fits into a groove and holds the shield in place. In one spot, there's a slight break in the clip that you can snag with the tip of the knife and pull inward. Be careful! The tiny clip is held in place by the groove, and as soon as you start to remove it, it will want to shoot across the room. When the clip is out, tap the bearing on a table, and the shield will drop right out. Now you can see all the tiny balls inside the bearing, and you can give them a good blast with the spray to clean them. After they've dried, add a drop of light oil and re-install the seal.

Droppin' Dogbones

I'm 14 years old and own a Futaba FX-10. It's a great, inexpensive, electric car. It's really durable and reliable for a beginner car. It has DuraTrax Gold competition shocks and a Trinity Slot Machine II motor. The car really flies on the road. It's a little bouncy in the back with its original shocks, but none of the aftermarket shocks will work with it, because the dogbones fall out going over the slightest bump.
DAVID DAVISON
Enterprise, AL

David, you can fix the dogbone problem very easily. The reason they fall out is because there's too much down-travel with the aftermarket units. To remedy this, add a piece of fuel tubing or hard plastic tubing on the shaft inside the shock body. This will prevent the rear arms from dropping too much. Build the new shocks, using the old ones as a guide for length. Cut two pieces of tubing of equal length, add one to each of the shocks' shafts and continue to assemble them, without oil.

If they're a good length, fill 'em up and go for it. You also might want to make sure the problem isn't that the shocks are too short when they're compressed. If this is the case, you can add tubing or small O-rings to the shock shaft outside the shock body.

Play Time's Over

I own a Tamiya Jaccs Civic front-wheel-drive sedan parking-lot racer. I've found that some of the suspension pivot areas, as well as the shocks, tend to be a little loose. I'd like to eliminate some of the slop: any suggestions? Also, I found that the rear end tends to slide out if I'm cornering really hard. Also, what do you recommend as hop-ups for this car?
BRETT WEIR
Kalamazoo, MI

Brett, I have some good tips for you. I was similarly disappointed with the fit of some of the parts on my front-wheel-drive car. My first solution was to ditch all the brass shock bushings. They just don't fit well, and they add slop to the suspension system. I took some Dynamite fuel line, jammed it through the top and bottom of each shock, and cut the line so a little sticks out on either side of the shock-mounting hole. Then, I pushed the stock mounting bolt back through and tightened the bolts so that the tubing is slightly compressed, but not too tight. Now there's no play in the suspension system.

I found another use for those brass shock bushings. I carefully drilled the suspension arms' inner hinge-pin holes and pressed the bushings into the arms. They fit a little more tightly than the stock setup, yet they still allow free movement. Another way I found to reduce slop in the steering was to add shock O-rings to the ball joints. Adding the O-rings to every ball joint before I snapped on the plastic link almost completely eliminated play in the steering system.

Besides bearings, the first hop-up I'd recommend is a set of stickier aftermarket tires. They should solve the rear traction problem.

CHAPTER 10

Masking Tricks

When spray-painting the inside of a Lexan body, you have to completely cover the outside of the body. I've tried masking tape and newspaper, but the paper tears or rips, and then I have to stop and fix it. What are the tricks of the trade for masking the outside of a Lexan body? Also, can I use graphic colored tape from an art-supply store for stripes? Thanks.
KEN HEITING
St. Petersburg, FL

Ken, for masking, try the clear plastic bag that came with the body. Flatten it out and apply masking tape to one edge, leaving about half the tape's width overlapping. Stick that overlapped tape to the bottom edge of the body, making sure to cover the whole side. At this point, to prevent a disaster, cover any body-post holes with masking tape. Fold the rest of the plastic bag over the body and tape the opposite side with more masking tape. Then just bunch up the excess plastic and tape it around the outside of the body. It seals well, and you can see how your paint job looks. As far as the graphic tape goes, you'll have to test it out yourself. I've used graphic line tape for thin black lines on the outside of a body with success, but brands might vary.

Tranny Trouble

I recently bought a Losi Double-X. I love the car, but I've been having an immense amount of trouble with the tranny. My problem is with the screw and locknut that hold the outdrive and the diff gear together. Every time I try to tighten the screw, it strips. But if it's too loose, it just sits there and winds out. Am I doing something wrong, or is this a problem that will always exist? Is there any way to fix it—like replacing the whole outdrive—or should I just replace the tranny? I'm hoping that you will be able to help me. You seem to know everything about these problems, and none of the hobby shops around here has been able to help me. Thank you for your time.
JARRED BELLROMINI
Galt, CA

Jarred, you should be able to get the screw tight enough to operate without stripping out the nut. I called Jack Johnson from Team Losi on this one, and he said that perhaps you have two of the bearings in the wrong place. The center diff bearing and the top shaft bearings look similar, but one is metric and one is standard. If you put the wrong one in the diff, you'll never get it tight enough, and you'll strip the nut trying. Swap the two, and you should be back in business!

Troubleshooting

Idle Conversation

I recently purchased an RC10GT with an O.S. CZ-R engine, and I have a couple of questions about tuning. I'm having an extremely hard time getting the engine to idle correctly. Mid-range and top end are great, but when I need the car to sit still for a second or two, it usually dies. The tuning instructions that came with the engine don't mention the low-end needle. Also, how critical is the length of the tuned pipe in regard to performance?
DJM, Spring, TX

The first thing you should check is the idle screw. Adjust it so the engine revs but doesn't cause the car to move. If that's OK, try leaning the low end by turning the screw in a click or two. Pinch the fuel line near the carb, and see whether the engine revs or fails. If it revs up, it's rich; if it dies, it's lean. Tuned-pipe length is important, but many people will argue whether the GT's pipe is tuned at all. Try altering the pipe length and note the changes you see. If you need more info, check out the "Pipe Basics" article in the April 1994 issue of Radio Control Car Action.

Help, I'm Melting...

I have a Team Associated RC10GT. The truck is great, but I have a problem with it. The idler gear in the Stealth transmission has melted twice. The transmission has bushings in it. Would adding ball bearings help, or do I just have to keep buying new idler gears all the time? Also, would MIP CVDs work in the RC10GT? Will the Traxxas Nitro Hawk body fit in this truck?
SEAN CORDOVA, Pueblo, CO

Sean, I've never heard of a problem like this, but it must have something to do with the bushings. Bushings create more drag than bearings, and they'll create more heat. If drag becomes excessive, it will melt the gear. Make sure that the bushings are well-lubed and that they allow the gear to spin freely. The best suggestion that I can make? Get a set of ball bearings; that should fix the problem! And yes, you can use MIP CVDs, and, with a little careful fitting, the Traxxas body will fit.

Index of Manufacturers

Airtronics, 11 Autry, Irvine, CA 92718; (714) 830-8769.

Associated Electrics Inc., 3585 Cadillac Ave., Costa Mesa, CA 92626; (714) 850-9342.

Blue Thunder; distributed by Horizon Hobby Distributors.

Bolink R/C Cars Inc., 420 Hosea Rd., Lawrenceville, GA 30245; (404) 963-0252.

Byron Originals, P.O. Box 279, Ida Grove, IA 51445; (712) 364-3165.

C&M/Team Cobra, P.O. Box 701-353, West Valley, UT 84170; (801) 974-5757.

Corally; distributed by Du-Mor R/C Inc., 1002 Union Landing Rd., Cinnaminson, NJ 08077; (609) 829-1338.

CRC, 6860 Stanwix Ave., Rome, NY 13440; (315) 338-0867.

Du-Bro Products, 480 Bonner Rd., P.O. Box 815, Wauconda, IL 60084; (708) 526-2136.

Dynamite; distributed by Horizon Hobby Distributors.

Flying Point; distributed by Racer's Choice R/C, P.O. Box 405, Medinah, IL 60157; (708) 980-4863.

Futaba Corp. of America, P.O. Box 19767, Irvine, CA 92713; (714) 455-9888.

Horizon Hobby Distributors, 4105 Fieldstone Rd., Champaign, IL 61821; (217) 355-9511.

Hyperdrive; distributed by PTI, P.O. Box 950, Pilot Mountain, NC 27401; (910) 368-1375.

JR; distributed by Horizon Hobby Distributors.

KO Propo; distributed by Great Planes Model Distributors, P.O. Box 9021, Champaign, IL 61826; (217) 398-3630.

Kyosho; distributed by Great Planes Model Distributors.

Litespeed, P.O. Box 4765, Spokane, WA 99202; (509) 535-2717.

McCoy Racing, 1778 Albright Ave., Upland, CA 91786.

McDaniel R/C, 1654 Crofton Blvd., Ste. 4, Crofton, MD 21114; (410) 721-6303.

MIP, 746 E. Edna Pl., Covina, CA 91723; (818) 339-9008.

MRC, P.O. Box 391, Edison, NJ 08818; (908) 248-0400.

Novak, 18910 Teller Ave., Irvine, CA 92715; (714) 833-8873.

O.S.; distributed by Great Planes Model Distributors.

Pactra; distributed by Testors Corp., 620 Buckbee St., Rockford, IL 61104.

Pirate; distributed by OFNA, 22600 D Lambert, Ste. 1009, Lake Forest, CA 92630; (714) 586-2910.

Raytek; distributed by Racer's Choice R/C.

Royal Products, 790 West Tennessee Ave., Denver, CO 80223; (303) 778-7711.

RPM, 14978 Sierra Bonita Ln., Chino, CA 91710; (909) 393-0366.

Schumacher Inc., 6302 Benjamin Rd., Ste. 404, Tampa, FL 33634; (813) 889-9691.

SCI, P.O. Box 13099, Airgate Station, Sarasota, FL 34278; (800) 673-9563.

Tamiya America Inc., 2 Orion, Aliso Viejo, CA 92656; (800) 826-4922.

Team Losi, 13848 Magnolia Ave., Chino, CA 91710; (909) 465-9400.

Tecnacraft, 200 Meadow View Dr., Grayson, GA 30221; (404) 995-1560.

Tekin Electronics, 940 Calle Negocio, San Clemente, CA 92673; (714) 498-9518.

Traxxas Corp., 12150 Shiloh Rd., #120, Dallas, TX 75228; (214) 613-3300.

Trinity Products Inc., 1901 E. Linden Ave., #8, Linden, NJ 07036; (908) 862-1705.

Yokomo Ltd., 25-2, Senju-Motomachi, Adachi-Ku, Tokyo 120, Japan.